Praise for *You Are Never Alone*

"Through heartfelt storytelling and the warm comfort of a pastor, Max assures us that we are stronger than we think because we have an ever-present source of help. The message of this book encourages us to find rest in God's powerful presence even amidst our darkest moments."

—Maria Shriver, *New York Times* bestselling
author and award-winning journalist

"If you ever question whether God cares deeply for you, open this book. Max reminds us that we are never without hope or help because we have a miracle-working God who walks alongside us and lifts us out of our storms."

—Bob Goff, *New York Times* bestselling author of *Love Does*
and *Everybody, Always*; creator of Dream Big Workshops

"My friend Max Lucado is one of the most trusted voices God has given this world. As usual, Max's timing is impeccable. Loneliness and isolation seem to be the root of so much of our pain. We are more digitally connected than ever, but our society feels lonelier by the day. Isn't it amazing to be reminded that we were created by God for relationship with him and that every inch and second of our fragile lives matter to him? Thank you, Max, for lifting our eyes up to this reality. I highly recommend this book."

—Chris Tomlin, artist, songwriter, author

"Loneliness is the new pandemic infecting our world. The statistics are staggering: 40 percent of all Americans say they lack meaningful relationships in their lives. The wonderful news is that none of us are really alone. We are loved by God and by more people than we may realize. Listen to the wisdom of my friend Max Lucado, a true American treasure, as he guides you into the best relationship you could ever have."

—Pastor Greg Laurie, senior pastor of Harvest Christian Fellowship,
author of *Johnny Cash: The Redemption of an American Icon*

"*You Are Never Alone* takes us beyond a cursory belief and invites readers into a life-giving belief—a belief that encourages us to place our full confidence in a living and loving Savior."

—Andy Stanley, founder and lead pastor of North
Point Ministries and author of *Irresistible*

"This is a beautiful, simple, faith-building book. Every page is so encouraging!"
—John Eldredge, *New York Times* bestselling author of *Wild at Heart*

"I have just finished reading Max Lucado's new book *You Are Never Alone*. I really enjoy the way he writes. Actually, he writes the way that Jesus spoke. It reaches where people live. He speaks the language of the common person and impacts our hearts in memorable ways. Thank you, Max, for just being who you are. Your thoughts touched me deeply and have encouraged me just where I needed it today. I highly recommend this book."
—Carter Conlon, General Overseer, Times Square Church Inc.

"God knew we needed this book. On the heels of a pandemic that isolated us and the ever-increasing rates of loneliness, this book gives the timely reminder that we are never alone. Max helps us open our eyes to the miracles all around us and provides great assurance that God is closer to us than we can ever imagine."
—Mark Batterson, *New York Times* bestselling author of *The Circle Maker* and lead pastor of National Community Church

"Max Lucado is a loving pastor and gifted communicator and we are extremely grateful for his friendship and ministry. *You Are Never Alone* is a divine invitation to a life of abundant and unyielding faith in our Savior—every chapter will undoubtedly lead you to a deeper confidence and trust in the promise that he is with you always."
—Brian and Bobbie Houston, global senior pastors, Hillsong Church

— YOU ARE —

Never Alone

Also by Max Lucado

SAN ANTONIO

The Hill Country of Texas is among the state's most beautiful assets. Great stretches of rolling hills are dotted with small farm communities and German villages that have changed little over the years. Rivers lined with oak, cedar, and cypress flow along the curves of the hills. You can drive for miles without seeing another car, yet a startled deer might dash across your path.

The hub of this part of Texas is San Antonio, a city rich in history. Although it is one of the largest cities in the United States, its past can still be glimpsed by foot, horse-drawn carriage, and river barge.

The Spanish first made camp along the banks of the river on June 13, 1691. Since it was the feast day of St. Anthony, they named the river San Antonio de Padua. Two decades later, Father Antonio Olivares built a mission here and named it San Antonio de Valero in honor of both the river and the viceroy of Spain.

Intended to convert the Indians to Christianity, this mission was to witness acts far from Christian, and its nickname was to become a rallying cry for Texas independence: In 1800 a contingent of Spanish soldiers added barracks to the complex of buildings at San Antonio de Valero and renamed it after their former quarters, San José y Santiago del Alamo de Parras—the Alamo.

The territory that was to become Texas came under the rule of Mexico after gaining independence from Spain. But the Mexican rule became oppressive, and by 1835 there were rumblings of revolution. In February, 1836, a group of 188 men, including Davy Crockett and Jim Bowie, barricaded themselves inside the Alamo. Their answer to the ultimatum of surrender ordered by Mexico's ruling dictator, General Antonio López de Santa Anna y Pérez, was a cannon shot. The Texans held off the Mexican army for twelve days. On the thirteenth, Santa Anna attacked with four thousand troops, killing everyone inside. But those thirteen days gave General Sam Houston enough time to rally his own army. He marched east, and forty-six days after the Alamo, he engaged Santa Anna's army at San Jacinto, near the present city of Houston. Eighteen minutes later, Sam Houston and his small army had defeated the Mexicans and won independence for Texas.

The Alamo, now under the direction of the Daughters of the Republic of Texas, has become a shrine, its stone walls and peaceful gardens creating a quiet spot in the heart of San Antonio's business district. There is, however, more to San Antonio than the Alamo. Four sister missions (Mission San Jóse, Mission Concepción, Mission San Juan Capistrano, and Mission San Francisco de la Espada) are now part of the Mission Trail, America's most complete mission complex, maintained under the National Park system.

The famous Riverwalk follows the San Antonio River through the downtown area. Lining the tree-shaded walk are dozens of shops and sidewalk cafés serving everything from tacos to quiche. Sightseeing barges regularly ply the waterways.

Just off the Riverwalk is La Villita (little town), a cobblestone street with restored adobe buildings. The Arneson River Theater is the setting for jazz, mariachis, and country-western bands. El Mercado, the old Mexican marketplace, dates back to 1840 and is still crowded with interesting shops. Towering over the area is the 750-foot Tower of the Americas, built for the 1968 HemisFair.

Just a few blocks from the river is the King William District. Built by wealthy German merchants in the 1870s and named for the King of Prussia, the neighborhood was originally a wide boulevard of Victorian mansions. It eventually grew into a twenty-five-block area that was the focal point of San Antonio society in the last decades of the nineteenth century. The Steves Homestead, one of the most beautiful in the area, is now a museum and is open for tours. During the Homes Tour in Fiesta Week, many private homes are also open.

San Antonio hosts a number of festivals and events throughout the year. Fiesta is a ten-day extravaganza in April. Brown Bag Days in June are highlighted by free entertainment in the city parks. In August, the Texas Folklife Festival gives visitors a chance to sample food, music, crafts, and dances of the dozens of ethnic groups in the area. In December, carolers stroll along the lighted Riverwalk, and the city is aglow with the Fiesta de las Luminarias.

Getting There: San Antonio is at the junction of two major interstate highways: I-10 and I-35. All major airlines fly into the international airport just north of the city.

The Rische House, a small two-story blue-and-gold Victorian dating from 1903, sits in the heart of San Antonio's King William District. It is run by Frances Bochat, a financial analyst for a local energy firm. A strong believer in B&Bs, she not only opened the first one in the area, but also operates a registry for other small establishments in the district.

The inn has only two guest rooms and a sleeping porch on the second floor. An outside stairway provides a private entrance to the rooms, which share a large bath with a claw-foot tub and old-fashioned shower. The front bedroom is quite large and airy, with a dormered ceiling and a king-size bed set in front of floor-to-ceiling windows. Done in peach with white accents, the room has a comfortable rattan chair and an antique knee-hole desk. The second bedroom, done in greens and pink, has twin beds, walls covered with art prints, and a bentwood rocker for evening reading.

RISCHE HOUSE

201 East Rische,
San Antonio, Texas 78204

Telephone: (512) 227-1190

Accommodations: two rooms with twin or king-size beds; shared bath with tub/shower; telephones available; television on sun porch.

Rates: moderate, Continental breakfast included. Children welcome. No pets.

Cards: AE, MC, V

No smoking. Open all year.

The sun porch, which was added on after the house was built, can be rented along with one of the bedrooms to accommodate an extra person. Otherwise, it is shared by all as a television and game room.

Before she leaves for work in the morning, Frances sets out breakfast in the tiny second-floor kitchen on complete settings of china and flatware. This meal usually consists of Mexican pastries from El Mercado, as well as cheese, fruit, English muffins, a selection of jams, and, of course, tea and coffee. In the evenings wine and sherry are available, and there are always snacks to munch on.

Guests are also welcome to use the small downstairs parlor, where white wicker and plants impart the feeling of a pleasant atrium. The small second-floor landing contains a selection of magazines for guests to browse through and two books on the King William District for those interested in a fascinating part of San Antonio history.

The inn is within walking distance of the Riverwalk, the Alamo, and shopping areas. On the last day of Fiesta Week, which commemorates the Battle of San Jacinto, is the King William Fair, featuring house tours in the district as well as crafts shows and food booths.

Getting There: Take the Commerce exit off Interstate 37, turn left on St. Mary's, cross Durango, and go another three blocks to South Alamo. Turn right on South Alamo, right on Guenther, left on Main, and right on Rische. The inn is on the right. There is a limousine service from the airport to the Four Seasons Hotel; Frances, like the other innkeepers in the King William District, will be happy to pick guests up there.

Carolyn Cole opened her B&B in the old Norton Brackenridge House and filled it with plants and family heirlooms. Antique English stained glass hangs in the windows, which are draped in long ruffled or lace curtains; the beds have hand-embroidered pillowcases and crocheted spreads. A family quilt lies at the foot of one bed, an aunt's hope chest at the foot of another.

The stately home, with four tall white columns supporting galleries on both floors, was built in 1903 by John T. Brackenridge, the nephew of the well-known philanthropist. Originally, the house stood in another part of the King William District, an elite San Antonio neighborhood. In 1935 it was converted into apartments, and then in 1984 moved to its present location. Two years later, Carolyn converted it into a bed-and-breakfast inn with four bedrooms.

Amid the heirlooms, Carolyn has sprinkled antiques picked up here and there, but it is the family touches that give the inn its character. Carolyn's aunt did the embroidery on the pillowcases, as well as the crocheted coverlet on one of the beds.

NORTON BRACKENRIDGE HOUSE BED AND BREAKFAST INN

230 Madison,
San Antonio, Texas 78204

Telephone: (512) 271-3442

Accommodations: four rooms with twin or queen-size beds; private baths with shower or tub/shower; telephones available; no television.

Rates: moderate, Continental breakfast included. Children welcome. Small pets allowed.

Cards: AE, MC, V

Closed Christmas Day.

The back bedroom has its own exit onto the porch and gardens. One of the front bedrooms is done in blue and white, the other in pink chintz. The rooms are minisuites, with kitchenettes (a legacy from apartment-house days) equipped with refrigerators and microwave ovens. Some of the rooms have baths with footed tubs and old-fashioned brass shower heads; others have a shower only.

The inn is filled with knickknacks: antique-looking porcelain pill jars on a dresser, a cottonseed-oil can from circa 1906 in one of the kitchens, and in another, parchment reproductions of the Constitution, which Carolyn bought during a childhood visit to Philadelphia. Some rooms have oil lamps and braided cloth baskets to hold magazines; all have wood floors.

Guests are served a Continental breakfast on trays in the upstairs foyer. The croissants are often topped with melted cheese, and there is always fruit, coffee, and juice. A basket of menus on the stairs provides help in choosing a restaurant for lunch or dinner.

From the second-floor landing there is access to the balcony, where guests may sit on the bent-willow furniture and enjoy the view of the restored Victorians that line the street. Shaded by pecan trees, the inn is within walking distance of the Alamo, La Villita, the Mexican market, and San Antonio's famous Riverwalk. And a trolley passes nearby on its way to downtown San Antonio.

Getting There: Take the Commerce Street exit off Interstate 37. Turn left on St. Mary's, cross Durango, go another two blocks to Madison, and turn right. The inn is on the right. Limousine service available from the airport for a fee.

Just outside the gates of Fort Sam Houston, the Bullis House stands in a part of San Antonio where tattoo shops and pool halls have sprung up around the still-active army post. The mansions, too expensive to keep as private homes, have for the most part been allowed to deteriorate over the years. As in many old neighborhoods, however, the residents are now beginning to realize the treasures they have in the old houses, which are slowly being restored.

The Bullis House was renovated several years ago for use as an international youth hostel. The first two floors of the mansion have now been made into a B&B, but the building next door is still used by hostelers.

The house was built in 1909 for General John Lapham Bullis, an Easterner who spent most of his army career in the Southwest. In 1873 he took command of a company of Seminole scouts, whose prowess at tracking and fighting Indian raiders attracted national attention. After Bullis retired in San Antonio, he engaged a noted

THE BULLIS HOUSE INN

621 Pierce Street, Box 8059, San Antonio, Texas 78208

Telephone: (512) 223-9426

Accommodations: seven rooms with twin or double beds; some with fireplaces; shared and private baths with tub or shower; no telephones; color television.

Rates: inexpensive, Continental breakfast included. Children welcome. No pets.

Cards: AE, MC, V

Meeting facilities. Texas Medallion. Open all year.

The Bullis House Inn

architect to build his family residence just outside the army post, but he died only two years after his new home was completed.

The white Neoclassic structure is still one of the most impressive buildings in the area, with tall columns and wide porches that spread out from both sides of the entrance. Inside, the sweeping, carved staircase is made of oak, and the floors have geometrically patterned borders of six different woods. Crystal chandeliers hang from ornate plaster medallions in the fourteen-foot ceilings, and the fireplaces are carved of either wood or marble. Even the basement has pressed-tin ceilings.

The Bullis mansion was the headquarters of an insurance company for a time, and it was probably during that period that the sprinkler system was installed; the pipes, now painted white to match the ceiling, still hang in full view. The mahogany woodwork was probably painted white at this time, too, though in some parts of the house it has been restored to its original state. Eventually the wainscoting in other parts of the house will also be restored.

All the original furniture had long been auctioned off by the time the house was renovated, so it is furnished comfortably rather than authentically. Overstuffed chairs and a sofa covered in bright chintz are clustered around the marble fireplace. The dining room, with its bay window and parqueted floors, is furnished with reproduction oak chairs and tables. Here, guests are served a Continental breakfast of juice, coffee, cold cereal, and warm fruit muffins; if they prefer, they may take their breakfast onto the veranda.

The downstairs guest room, done in blue and white, is the only one with a private bath and one of four rooms with fireplaces, this one mirrored and bricked. Swagged drapes hang in the windows over the bed. Against another wall is a reproduction brass and white-iron daybed covered in white eyelet.

Upstairs, six rooms encircle the wide landing. One room has been done in a 1930s style, with a modern rollaway in addition to the double bed. Another room has a carved bed, rattan chair, and blue-tiled fireplace. The inside corner room is quiet and bright with rattan furniture, pink tiles on the fireplace, and mauve walls. Several rooms have tall windows that open onto small verandas, which no longer have railings—another alteration by the insurance company. Even on the hottest days, a cool cross breeze flows through the house.

Getting There: Take Interstate 35 north to exit 159A. Turn left onto New Braunfels and go over the freeway. Turn left on Grayson and left again on Pierce. The inn is on the corner of Grayson and Pierce.

In 1894 Edwin Holland Terrell built this turreted house on Grayson Street as a wedding gift for his bride. During the four years he spent in Europe as United States Ambassador to Belgium, he had become fascinated with castles. When he returned to San Antonio, he commissioned noted architect Alfred Giles to design a home that would be a mixture of German castle and French château.

He named it Lambermont in honor of a friend, and the castle served as the family residence until Terrell's death in 1908. Among the twenty-six rooms were a library with glassed-in bookcases, a parlor, a music room, a solarium, a wine cellar, and a ballroom.

Alice Longworth Roosevelt lived here for a while, as did one of President Mc-Kinley's daughters. At one time you could have your fortune told in the front parlor, but people came more out of curiosity about the building than to see the fortune teller who lived there. A Mrs. Samuels bought the house in the mid-1950s, modernized it, and turned the numerous bedrooms into apartments.

In 1986 present owners Katherine Poulis and her daughter Nancy Haley took a trip to Utah. While in Provo, they found that all the motels were booked and their only option was a B&B, something they had never considered before. After returning home, they realized that the one part of the trip they kept talking about was their stay at the bed-and-breakfast inn. A few weeks later, they heard that Lambermont was for sale. The real estate agent kept apologizing for the number of bathrooms in the house, but it gave Katherine and Nancy the same idea: bed and breakfast.

They bought the castle in April of 1986 and began renovating it. Fortunately, the place was in good condition and needed mostly minor repairs like cleaning mildewed woodwork and cutting down the overgrown bamboo and magnolias that hid the castle from the street.

Throughout the house they found beveled glass, inlaid wood floors, and nine carved and tiled fireplaces—but not one light fixture. Chandeliers were purchased, and swagged drapes and sheers were custom made for the dozens of tall windows. Furniture, however, was no problem. Both women had sold their large homes and between them they managed to fill the castle almost entirely with three or four generations of family pieces.

The entry hall, once all dark wood, at some point in its long history was painted white with gilt touches. In one corner there is an inglenook, and the gilt mirror on the wall, inherited by Katherine's mother, is even older than the house.

TERRELL CASTLE

950 East Grayson Street,
San Antonio, Texas 78208

Telephone: (512) 271-9145
or 824-8036

Accommodations: nine rooms with twin, double, or king-size beds; several with fireplaces; private and shared baths with shower or tub/shower; telephones available; television in suites.

Rates: moderate, full breakfast included. Children welcome. Pets allowed in dog run at the back of the castle.

Cards: MC, V

Meeting facilities. Open all year.

3/15/91
Reservation
3rd Floor
w/ Kip + Kelly

Terrell Castle

The parlor, with its tiled and mirrored fireplace, has an antique hide-a-bed and a leather-topped coffee table. The formal dining room and a small meeting-room-cum-gift-shop are across the hall.

Of the nine bedrooms in the castle, six are on the second floor, two on the third, and one on the fourth. Some have beveled mirrors and bay windows, and most have their own fireplaces, which have been converted to gas. The former kitchenettes are now dressing rooms and wet bars. All the rooms in the house are quite large, and those over the front between the turrets are octagonal. Furniture ranges from antique headboards and mirrored bookcases to modern reproductions.

The best room, and one of the last to be renovated, is the Americana Room on the fourth floor above the old ballroom. From its windows, which open in the directions of the four cardinal points of the compass, guests have a 360-degree view of San Antonio. The antique wooden bed sits on a red carpet, surrounded by blue enamel furniture. An old potbellied stove from Fredericksburg keeps you warm on winter nights, and the view is worth the inconvenience of a bath one flight down.

Katherine and Nancy serve a full breakfast in the formal dining room. The menu usually includes ham, bacon, or sausage, eggs, hash browns, grits, and baked goods like biscuits or dill bread with an assortment of jellies and jams.

When the Terrell Castle was finally ready for guests, Katherine and Nancy turned the long-awaited grand opening into a scholarship benefit for San Antonio's Baptist Medical Center, where both women are department directors. Since Terrell is a well-known name in San Antonio, they renamed the castle. Descendants of both Terrell and architect Alfred Giles attended the ceremonies.

Getting There: Take Interstate 35 north to exit 159A. Turn left onto New Braunfels and go over the freeway. Turn left on Grayson and go about three blocks. Inn is on the left.

BANDERA

Bandera, Texas, is the Cowboy Capital of the World, and a monument on the Courthouse lawn proclaims it the home of seven world-champion cowboys. There are reportedly ten million miles of deer trails in the area, and not one foot of railroad.

An hour west of San Antonio, Bandera is a quiet little town, except perhaps on Saturday night, when guests from the surrounding dude ranches come to sample the frontier night life in the Western taverns and dance halls that line the main street.

During the day, those not out riding the range can shop in the Western-wear stores or visit the Frontier Times Museum, the Old Jail Museum, the Stanislaus

Catholic Church, and the Bandera County Courthouse. Old Camp Verde, once a camel outpost, is just across the county line in Kerr County—and just south of town there are dinosaur tracks. The Chamber of Commerce will provide visitors with a self-guided walking tour of town.

The area around Bandera is mostly ranch country. The rugged hills spawn clear, fresh streams that run into the Medina River. Favorite pastimes include canoeing on the river, float trips down the rapids, and swimming. Nearby Medina Lake offers fishing, boating, and water skiing. The Hill Country State Natural Area, long a mecca for hikers, now has riding trails for those who have their own horses; camping facilities are available. There are two golf courses, two rodeo arenas, and a horse racetrack in the area. Lost Maples State Park is also nearby.

Located halfway between San Antonio and Kerrville, Bandera is primarily a tourist community. A Funtier Days Celebration is held on Memorial Day, and the Hunter's Barbecue, when the town usually feeds about two thousand people on the night before the opening day of deer- and turkey-hunting season, takes place in November. The Cowboy Capital Trail Ride to San Antonio is in February.

But activities aside, the area's greatest asset is its setting. Huge cypress, pecan, and elm trees border the Medina River, and the ranch lands are covered with live oak, cedar, wild cherry, mountain laurel, and cactus. Wildlife—Russian boar, javelina, dove, quail, squirrel, and deer, to name a few—is abundant in the area. There are also private game ranches with exotic African and Asian animals.

Getting There: Bandera is 40 miles west of San Antonio on Highway 16.

The Dixie Dude Ranch, one of the oldest in the area, opened on July 3, 1937, and since then five generations of the Whitley family have welcomed guests. The 1,700-acre ranch was bought for back taxes in 1901 by William Wallace Whitley. The original homestead, now long gone, was down behind a stand of oaks not far from the present ranch buildings. As a reminder of the rough-and-tumble years of the last century, an old grave nearby, now newly marked, commemorates the spot where two men died in a range war.

In 1937 Whitley decided to open the ranch to guests and asked his daughter Billie and her husband, Dee Crowell, to help run the dude ranch. During World War II the guests were mostly servicemen sent there to recuperate from their wounds. One of the convalescents stayed on and was the town doctor for nearly forty years.

The Dixie Dude is a working ranch now run by Clay Conoly, Billie's grandson and a fourth-generation dude rancher. He has recently given the place a face-lift,

DIXIE DUDE RANCH

Box 548,
Bandera, Texas 78003

Telephone: (512) 796-4481

Accommodations: twenty rooms with twin or double beds; some rooms with fireplaces; private baths with shower or tub/shower; no telephones; television available.

Rates: moderate, all meals, one horseback ride, and all activities included. Children welcome. Pets discouraged.

Cards: MC, V

Open all year.

repainting, repairing, and adding new drapes and bedspreads to the rooms. Some of the cabins have been completely rebuilt.

Since families and groups comprise the greatest percentage of guests, the rooms are all simply furnished and set up family style with two or more beds. Some rooms are quite large, others have one large bedroom and an adjoining small bedroom or sleeping porch. Some have tile floors, and most of the baths have both tubs and showers.

Food is plentiful and good: meat-and-potatoes fare served family style at long tables, giving guests a chance to get acquainted. After a while, many of them begin to feel like family. That Western flavor and the genuine hospitality is the reason guests come back year after year, some from as far away as Switzerland, Norway, France, Germany, and Sweden. One woman has been coming to the ranch every year since Labor Day, 1941.

Rates include lodging, three meals a day, one horseback ride each day, and swimming in the large pool. The staff arranges cookouts, poolside parties, and barbecues. There is also volleyball, croquet, and table tennis. The Round-up Room at the ranch headquarters has a television, a jukebox, and a piano. Comfortable chairs and couches are clustered around the stone fireplace, and there's plenty of room for dancing.

On days when there are no rides scheduled, the staff will take guests on afternoon excursions around Bandera, Kerrville, and other neighboring towns. In the evenings, you can sit around the campfire and listen to old Western songs or watch one of the local men perform rope tricks.

As at any guest ranch, everyone spends most of their time outdoors, and this is a particularly beautiful part of Texas for that. The rolling hills stretch to the horizon, and giant, spreading live oaks provide welcome shade in the hot summer and protection from the rain in winter. The picturesque old barn, now weathered to a soft gray, still stands behind the guest quarters, and if you know where to look, you'll find dinosaur tracks down by the river.

Getting There: Coming from San Antonio on Highway 16, turn left on Highway 173 in Bandera, go half a mile to Highway 1077, and turn right. The ranch is 9 miles down, on the left.

The Silver Spur Guest Ranch is the newest and smallest of the guest ranches in the Bandera area. Built in 1980 by Tom Winchell (because he had enjoyed stays at guest ranches as a youth), it borders the five thousand acres of the Hill Country State Natural Area.

The ranch house is built of native stone in a traditional style, with dormered second-story windows and a roof that slopes down in front to form the roof of the long, wide porch. The grounds around the main house and stone cabins are wide open. It seems as if you can see for miles.

The inside of the main lodge is positively cavernous. One of the two enormous rooms is a gathering spot, with video games, a player piano, and a pool table at one end, and a large stone fireplace and a cluster of couches and chairs at the other. The rolltop desk that serves as the office and guest register is at the back. Leaded-glass windows look out to the porch and the view beyond. The other room is the dining area, with a brick floor and long wooden tables. The massive support posts are hung with boots, spurs, and other cowboy paraphernalia.

Upstairs a general store sells country clothes and souvenirs, and there are guest rooms up here as well. The two end rooms are large and light with a country look: dormered windows, ruffled curtains, and beds topped with quilted coverlets. The interior rooms are smaller and have no windows.

Most guest rooms, however, are in small stone cottages scattered about the grounds. Each is named for a historic character from the Wild West: Jesse James, Wyatt Earp, Doc Holiday, Belle Starr, Butch Cassidy and the Sundance Kid, even Lillie Langtry and Judge Roy Bean.

The two-room cottages are roomy and have large baths, wood paneling, brick floors, and double or king-size beds. A small hallway connects the rooms so they can be made into a suite. All have porches with views, and in the evening and early morning you can catch a glimpse of white-tailed deer, wild turkey, and javelina.

The ranch specializes in riding and offers three or more hours of horseback riding each day. If you don't know how to ride, the staff will teach you. If you are already a good rider, you can take treks into the state natural area.

Between rides the staff arranges cookouts; a morning ride includes a stop for breakfast tacos and tortillas, fried potatoes, sausage and eggs, fruit, and sweet rolls. Every Saturday night there's a Texas barbecue under the live oaks and cedars. A couple of times each week guests are treated to events like Western dances.

SILVER SPUR GUEST RANCH

Box 1657,
Bandera, Texas 78003

Telephone: (512) 796-3639

Accommodations: eleven rooms with double or king-size beds; private baths with tub/shower; no telephones; color television.

Rates: moderate, three meals and two horseback rides per day included. Children welcome. No pets.

Cards: MC, V

Open all year.

Silver Spur Guest Ranch

Hiking, volleyball, and table tennis are available on the ranch, and since the 275 acres do not border the Medina River, there is a junior Olympic pool for water activities. Guests go into town to rent equipment for float trips or canoeing on the river, or to play golf or tennis.

The ranch is eleven miles from Bandera, down a country road that becomes a dirt road for the last two miles. Just to remind everyone to close the gate, there is a "cowboy's grave" at the entrance—a pile of stones with boots sticking out and a tombstone that states: "R.I.P. Here lies the last S.O.G. that didn't shut the gate."

Getting There: Coming from San Antonio on Highway 16, turn left at the Texaco station (Highway 173) and go one-half mile; then turn right on Highway 1077. The ranch is 10 miles down Highway 1077 on the left (the last mile or so is dirt road). Turn into the gate and drive another mile to the ranch house. Transportation is available from the "Flying L" airstrip.

The Medina River forms a horseshoe around the Mayan Dude Ranch. In fact, to get to the ranch you must drive over a narrow bridge, the rushing water just inches below your tires. Across the river, the wooded area opens to a pasture with grazing horses and reminders all along the road that the horses, not the cars, have the right-of-way. In the ranch complex itself, the horses find colorful competition in some hundred peacocks that roam the wooded areas.

The staff gives you a map when you check in, and with good reason; it would be very easy to get lost between the dining room and your cabin. The Hicks Gang (Don, his wife Judy, and their thirteen kids) run the ranch, which was built in about 1930 as a Girl Scout Camp. You can still see the logo emblazoned on the stone fireplace in the main ranch house. It was owned for a time by Dr. Binkley, the infamous "goat gland" doctor; in 1951, Don Hicks' father bought the place.

There is a two-day minimum stay at the ranch, and during the summer activities are planned on a weekly basis. For instance, Sunday is softball and barbecue day. On Monday you can learn western dancing after the steak fry. Tuesday is Irish night, and mariachi music fills the air on Wednesday. Thursday brings gangsters and Keystone Kops, and Friday, the Grand Old Opry. Saturday you can dance to the tunes of the 50's. Between activities there are treks to Booger Red's Saloon at Mayan City, the "ghost town" on the ranch. And what dude ranch would be complete without trail rides? Horseback riding is the only activity you must sign

MAYAN DUDE RANCH
Box 577,
Bandera, Texas 78003

Telephone: (512) 796-3312
or 796-3036

Accommodations: sixty rooms with twin, double, queen-, or king-size beds; some rooms with fireplaces; private baths with tub/shower; no telephones; television available.

Rates: expensive (weekly rates and children's rates available), all meals included. Children welcome. No pets.

Cards: AE, CB, DC, MC, V

Limited wheelchair access. Open all year.

up for, and two rides a day (except Sunday in the busy season) are included in the room rate. Children have their own supervised activities like piñata-breaking contests, coloring contests, and watermelon hunts.

Coffee and juice are brought to your door in the morning; you then have the option of eating in the dining hall, or taking a breakfast ride (or a hayride) to the cookout for eggs, grits, hash browns, bacon, homemade sausage, biscuits, and breakfast tortillas and tacos. For lunch, you can choose the salads, fresh fruit, and wine that are served poolside at the Swim Corral, or a more substantial meat-and-potatoes meal available in the dining room.

During the months when the regular set of activities is not offered, the ranch still provides a variety of events, though not as rigidly scheduled or as diverse as in season. In the off season, from October to May, the ranch offers Wild West Weekends: You check in Friday and take a hayride to the Medina River patio for a barbecue, ride and lounge on Saturday, and then top off the weekend with a prime-rib dinner and an evening in the gambling parlor.

The accommodations at the ranch are geared for families, which make up the majority of the guests. Three lodges and a cluster of stone cottages are scattered about the woods so everyone has privacy. Some rooms are decorated like jails, others like gold mines or treehouses. Other rooms have beds with wagon-wheel headboards and kick-post footboards, cowboy-statue lamps, and lacquered pine furniture. Some of the rooms also have fireplaces.

Suites are available in the main lodge. The Log Inn has connecting rooms, one with two double beds, the other with one king-size bed. Loft units, ideal for two families traveling together, have two bedrooms and two baths, with a living area and a loft for the kids to sleep in.

There are seminar facilities and meeting rooms for seventy. The Trading Post Souvenir Shop is open daily. A saloon in the main lodge has a wide deck overlooking the river and the valley, or you can ride your horse over to Booger Red's Saloon.

One of the highlights of a stay at the ranch is innertubing down the river. You'll also find an old-fashioned "swimmin' hole," hiking, and fishing for catfish, bass, and perch. A nine-hole golf course is nearby.

Getting There: From San Antonio, take Highway 16 into Bandera. Turn right at the stoplight, go three blocks, and turn left at Pecan Street. Go across the river to the Main Lodge. Airport service is available from "Flying L" in Bandera, and from San Antonio for a fee.

Eight miles outside the small hill town of Boerne (pronounced "Bernie") lies the Guadalupe River Ranch. The president of the Alamo National Bank built the place for entertaining in the late 1920s. A decade later, the idyllic setting, on a cliff 180 feet above the Guadalupe River, was the private retreat of Olivia de Havilland. The eight-thousand-square-foot main house, built of native limestone, has forty-eight handhewn beams in the ceilings, a stone fireplace in each of the large rooms, hardwood floors, and only two bedrooms.

The ranch itself was put together from pieces of three other ranches around a three-mile horseshoe bend in the Guadalupe River. The original owner built stone walls around the immediate four acres and planted oak trees, now sixty years old, in soil brought up from the valley. After a few years he sold the ranch to Olivia de Havilland, who also stayed only a few years. In the early 1960s it was turned into a guest ranch. Finally, in the late 1970s, Guadalupe River Ranch was purchased and restored by Walter Starcke, Broadway actor, producer, director, author, and lecturer. Starcke's original plan was to make the ranch into an art community, and until recently the resort accepted only groups. Overnight guests are now welcome.

The three hundred acres of ranch land extend only as far as the cypress-lined river, but on a clear day you can see three ridges of hills in the distance. So spectacular is the view that an observation deck with a swing was built at the edge of the cliff. Throughout the area are stone walkways and immaculate flower beds; another stone path leads through the woods and down to the river.

The main house is the community area with dining room, solarium, and sitting and meeting areas. On cold, blustery days a roaring fire burns in the fireplace, around which couches and wing chairs are clustered.

Guests stay in small cottages scattered around the bluff. Some have screened sleeping porches, butler's pantries, or private patios; all are carpeted, heated, and air-conditioned. The walls are limestone, inside and out, and the furniture simple and comfortable, as befits the setting. All the cottages are named for people who have influenced Starcke in some way: Walt Whitman, Georgia O'Keeffe, Albert Einstein, Carl Jung. These particular cottages are grouped around a small courtyard with a wishing well. Besides the cottages, there is a new two-story building with views of the river, as well as a spa area with economy accommodations.

The chefs can prepare anything from a gourmet dinner to vegetarian fare to old-fashioned Texas barbecue, but generally the food is Continental or Southwestern. The main dining room has a beamed ceiling, fireplace, and view of the distant hills. If you prefer, you can dine in the solarium, which is furnished with Mexican pigskin chairs and tile tables.

GUADALUPE RIVER RANCH

Box 929,
Boerne, Texas 78006

Telephone: (512) 537-4837

Accommodations: twenty-six rooms with twelve dorms, with twin, double, or queen-size beds; private baths at ranch, shared in dorm rooms, with tub/shower; telephones available on request; television in main-house lounge.

Rates: expensive to very expensive, all meals included. Children welcome. No pets.

Cards: MC, V

Open all year.

There is plenty to do here; the ranch has tennis courts, an Olympic-size swimming pool, whirlpool bath, nature trails, a volleyball court, and croquet on the lawn. There's also swimming, fishing, and innertubing in the Guadalupe River. One of the original buildings, now called the Will Rogers, is used as a museum. Made of stones and sod, it shows how frontier people lived in the last century.

The German heritage of the town of Boerne is evident from the architecture: stone buildings, narrow windows, steep gables, and outside staircases. The town was laid out to resemble communities the founders had known in Europe. Among the things to see in the area are Cascade Caverns, with a ninety-foot underground waterfall, Cave Without a Name, and Natural Bridge Cave and Wildlife Park. The area also offers horseback riding. Deer can be seen year round on the ranch, and in the fall the oaks put on a display of red that is truly spectacular.

Getting There: Take Interstate 10 to Boerne and Business 87 into town. Go through four stoplights and turn left on FM 474. Go 8 miles to the entrance of the ranch; it's another mile to the complex. Transportation is available, with advance notice, from San Antonio International Airport, 28 miles away.

Bob Steinruck was working for an oil company in Venezuela when he and his wife, Carol, bought Lazy Hills in 1959—sight unseen. Located eight miles outside of Kerrville, the ranch was called the Lazy H Dude Ranch in the 1940s. It became a boys' camp for a while, and in the 1970s was a school. Today it is a guest ranch again, as well as a working ranch with cattle, horses, and hogs. Bob and Carol run it with the help of their children. Their daughter does the cooking, their son runs the horse operation, and a daughter-in-law handles the front desk.

The guest rooms are housed in small cottages of native stone built around the main lodge. They are decorated in Western style, and some of the handcrafted furniture has been there since the 1940s. The twin beds have wagon-wheel headboards and kick-post footboards, blue denim bedspreads, and bright red blankets. Drawer handles on the bureaus are fashioned like tiny stirrups, and the mirrors are framed with horse collars. Six of the rooms have fireplaces. Hill House, which as the name implies sits high on a hill, has two rooms with six beds in each and a living room with a fireplace; it's ideal for small groups. A new wing, added in 1978, contains more modern rooms with king-size beds and large dressing areas.

Horseback riding is not included in the room rate unless guests have booked for an entire week. The staff, however, does arrange Texas cookouts, hayrides, and trail rides through the 750-acre ranch.

LAZY HILLS GUEST RANCH

Box I, Ingram, Texas 78025

Telephone: (512) 367-5600

Accommodations: twenty-five rooms with twin or queen-size beds; some with fireplaces; private baths with shower; no telephones; television in lounge.

Rates: inexpensive, all meals included. Weekly rates include horseback riding. Children welcome. No pets.

Cards: MC, V

No smoking in the dining room. Wheelchair access. Open all year.

There is also an Olympic-size pool, a hot tub, lighted tennis courts, volleyball and basketball courts, and shuffleboard. Inside there's a game room with billiards and table tennis. The ranch caters to kids, too: There's a tree house, a merry-go-round, and a stagecoach frame to climb on. The ranch has more than thirty miles of trails and two ponds, one stocked with bass, the other with farm-fed catfish.

The dinner bell (from an old schoolhouse in Pennsylvania where Bob's mother once taught) calls guests to meals three times a day. The hearty Western fare is served family style in the dining room at tables that seat eight. Breakfast is substantial, with hotcakes, eggs, and sausage. Lunch is likely to be something like spaghetti, and dinner is usually old-fashioned steak and potatoes.

The setting is not only beautiful, but also peaceful. The porches all have chairs for sitting and admiring the surrounding hills, which turn a soft reddish color in the fall. There are also hummingbirds by the hundreds. You'll find lots to do in Kerrville: Summer Theater, the Memorial Day Music Festival, Labor Day Bluegrass Festival, and the Goodtime Music Festival held Columbus Day weekend.

Getting There: Take Interstate 10 into Kerrville. Take Highway 27 west to Ingram, turn right at the stoplight and drive two and a half miles to the Lazy Hills sign on the right. Airport transportation from Kerrville is available.

FREDERICKSBURG

Fredericksburg was founded by German immigrants on May 8, 1846, and named for the highest ranking member of the Adelsverein (Society of Nobility), Prince Frederick of Prussia. It was under the auspices of this society that these German settlers had come west to the New World.

Each family was given a lot in town and a tract of land in the country to farm. All week they worked the land; then on Saturday they came into town to buy necessities and sell crops. Many built one-room houses on their town lots, usually with an outside staircase to a sleeping loft. The family would stay there Saturday night and attend church on Sunday morning, hence the name "Sunday house."

When the settlers came to the area, it was Indian territory, and one delightful story from these early times has become a cherished tradition: One evening, when Indians were camped on the hillsides around the settlement, a pioneer mother told her frightened children that the fires were built by the Easter Bunny so he could cook his colored eggs. Now, at Easter time, bonfires are lit on the hillsides in an annual celebration enjoyed by citizens and visitors, adults and children alike.

The town still retains its German heritage. There is more strudel than chili, and as in any self-respecting German community, the bakeries tempt and delight. Instead of the Victorian structures common elsewhere in Texas, Fredericksburg is comprised of square, serviceable stone buildings. Many, like Vereins Kirche, date back to the mid-nineteenth century. This eight-sided church was built in 1847.

One of the most unusual structures in town is the steamboat-shaped Hotel Nimitz, built in 1852 by Captain Charles Nimitz (grandfather of Fleet Admiral Chester W. Nimitz, who was born in Fredericksburg in 1885). Converted into a museum in 1966, the year the admiral died, the hotel has been dedicated to all who served under him in World War II. The Garden of Peace behind the hotel was a gift from the people of Japan.

Just seventy miles from both San Antonio and Austin, Fredericksburg is a favorite getaway spot for city dwellers. There is a nine-hole golf course in nearby Lady Bird Johnson Park, and a year-long calendar of events. Fredericksburg is the site of the oldest county fair in Texas, and is also known as the Peach Tree Capital of Texas; the citizens celebrate the peach harvest every year. The Easter Fires Pageant is held every spring, followed by Founders Day, a Memorial Day horse race, a Fourth of July race festival, and Night in Old Fredericksburg in July. No German community would omit Octoberfest, and there is a candlelight tour of the historic homes in December.

Getting There: Fredericksburg is deep in the Hill Country, 68 miles northwest of San Antonio via Interstate 10 west to Highway 87 north. It's 70 miles west of Austin via Highway 290.

Baron's Creek and Town Creek established the original boundaries of Fredericksburg. In 1880 Max Eckert built a Sunday house on his land, just across the way from Baron's Creek. He added a kitchen later, moved the Sunday house to the back of the lot, and then added a "car house" (garage).

The main house, like the Sunday house, was added onto over the years. Built of "basse block," the main house has three gables and porches accented with handmade gingerbread woodwork. The date of the original construction, 1911, is imprinted above the front door, and "Eckert" is stamped in the concrete step. Now part of the National Historic District of Fredericksburg, the old house until recently was rented out as apartments by Eckert's two daughters.

Renovations for a B&B included stripping the linoleum to reveal lodgepole pine floors and repainting the army-green walls in soft pastels.

BARON'S CREEK INN

110 East Creek Street,
Fredericksburg, Texas 78624

Telephone: (512) 997-9398

Accommodations: five suites with queen-size beds; private baths with footed tub and shower; no telephones; television in rooms.

Rates: expensive, fancy Continental breakfast included. Children over ten welcome. No pets.

Cards: MC, V

No smoking. Open all year.

Baron's Creek Inn

The four three-room suites all have private baths, as does the Sunday house. Each suite is filled with plants and furnished with antiques. Fully equipped kitchens contain small refrigerators and microwave ovens for those who wish to prepare their own meals or bring back treats from the plethora of bakeries in town.

The downstairs suites in the main house are done in blues, greens, and mauves, and each has a four-poster bed. The second-story suite on the east side is done in gray highlighted with brown, white, pink, and green. Solid oak antiques are mixed with rattan chairs and Chinese carpets. On the west side of the house, a suite done in browns and peach hues has its own private entrance. The Sunday House has a beveled-glass door off its own covered porch. The rock floor is now surfaced with wooden planks, the walls are sheathed in bead board, and the use of lace, eyelet, and chintz reminds one of a summer cottage.

Breakfast is a fancy Continental affair served at your door. It includes things like breakfast sausage roll, bakery pastries, and fresh fruit. Each suite has its own coffee maker. On pleasant mornings, most guests carry their breakfasts to the wrought-iron tables and chairs on the porch overlooking the gardens, which are shaded by pecan trees and filled with flowers. To get the key to your room, you must check in downtown at 402 West Main before 9 p.m.

Getting There: Take Interstate 10 to Comfort, then go north on Highway 87 to Fredericksburg. Turn left on Main Street, left on Llano, and left again on Creek. The inn is on the left. Transportation available from the municipal airport.

Check-in here, as at Baron's Creek Inn, is a bit different from most B&Bs. There is no live-in manager or owner, so you must go down Main Street a few blocks to the Country Cottage Antiques store to get your key. But on your arrival, you'll find complimentary wine left in your room, as well as rolls from a nearby German bakery for your breakfast.

There are two suites and two guest rooms in the inn; a fifth unit is located in a loft area over the antiques store in a building known as the Hencke House, the birthplace of Admiral Chester W. Nimitz. Since the inn is associated with an antiques shop, the rooms are naturally filled with an array of unusual furnishings and accessories. Among the amenities provided are his-and-hers French bathrobes and engraved glasses, both of which can be purchased in the shop.

The inn itself is a two-story stone building with a white wooden balcony. The rafters were hand cut from local cypress and the interior walls are whitewashed adobe. The two front rooms were built in 1850, only four years after Fredericksburg

COUNTRY COTTAGE INN

405 East Main Street,
Fredericksburg, Texas 78624

Telephone: (512) 997-8549

Accommodations: five rooms with double or king-size beds; private baths with tub, shower, or tub/shower; telephone in community kitchen; television in rooms.

Rates: moderate, serve-yourself Continental breakfast included. Children welcome. No pets.

Cards: MC, V

No smoking inside the inn. Texas Medallion. Open all year.

was founded (the structure was the first two-story house in town). Another four rooms were added ten years later, and the kitchen was built in 1950.

The Oak Suite, decorated in blues and browns, has a working fireplace in the sitting room and a huge whirlpool bath in what was once the dining room. The sitting room is done in Early American reproduction furniture, with French accents such as a bellows, circa 1838, for a table. Above the fireplace is a flint-embedded board used by the French to separate grain from chaff. The king-size bed is set against a large window, and there is a German wardrobe.

The Pecan Room has an Amish quilt above the beds, a spindle-back rocker, and leaded doors from an old mission in San Antonio. The sunny Cypress Room is done in blues, with curved lintels over the doors and a whirlpool tub.

The Cedar Suite has two bedrooms and a private bath, an entrance from the upstairs balcony, an open-beamed ceiling, and wood floors. A French winnowing basket filled with dried flowers hangs over the wooden headboard. There is also a French crib and an Early American "hired hand's bed." The Nimitz Room, part of the Cedar Suite, is so named because all the furniture in the room came from the Hencke House.

The fifth room, the Mountain Laurel, is above the Hencke House. Reached by an outside staircase, this loft area over the antiques store has a pitched roof with open beams and is decorated with rustic country furniture; the braided rugs on the wood floor were made by Admiral Nimitz's aunt. The small kerosene stove is just for show, but the microwave oven and the coffee maker are for guests' use. The "private" bath consists of an eight-foot copper tub that sits under a skylight in the room, and a toilet hidden behind a curtain.

The inn has a Texas Medallion and is part of the National Historic District.

Getting There: Take Interstate 10 west to Comfort and Highway 87 north to Main. Turn right onto Main; the inn is about half a block down on the right. To check in, turn left on Main and go about two blocks to the Country Cottage Antiques Shop at 247 East Main. (Arrival after 5 p.m. is by special arrangement only.) Transportation available from municipal airport with advance notice.

HIGHLAND LAKES AREA

The original inhabitants of this fertile lake area north of San Antonio were the Indians, and artifacts from their centuries-long habitation of this land are on display at the Llano County Museum. The Spanish were here as early as 1535, but the Germans, who came in the mid-nineteenth century, were the first Europeans to settle here.

The Germans came to Indian territory under the auspices of the Adelsverein, the Society of Nobility. A treaty with the Comanches opened the land to settlers, yet life here was not without its dangers. The last battle between Texans and Comanches occurred in 1873, a few miles east of Llano on Packsaddle Mountain.

In the 1880s the discovery of a large deposit of magnetic iron ore in the area made Llano a boomtown overnight, but the absence of coal, necessary for making steel, made that boom short lived. Then, in 1888, J. K. Finlay polished the first piece of Llano granite. Subsequently, over twelve varieties of granite were quarried in six operations, which peaked in 1935. Nearby Marble Falls also produced granite, some of which went into building the State Capitol in Austin and the Galveston Seawall, among other structures.

The town of Marble Falls, situated near the spot where the Colorado River cascades over the granite in several spectacular falls, has the distinction of being the only American city laid out by a blind man. In 1886 General Adam Johnson, blinded in the Civil War, plotted and surveyed the town site.

The Highland Lakes, which boast 450 miles of shoreline, are the main attraction of this part of Texas. These crystal-blue lakes offer fishing, boating, and other water sports. Pearls of rare quality have even been found in the fresh-water mussels along the Colorado River.

Visitors can take the Vanishing Texas River Cruise, named for the Texas River, which disappears into Lake Buchanan. From November to March, bald eagles, white-tailed deer, wild turkeys, great blue herons, crested cormorants, kingfishers, and feral hogs inhabit the area. Nearby are Longhorn Cavern State Park and Enchanted Rock State Natural Area, an outcropping of pink granite.

Throughout the area you'll find golf, tennis, and camping, as well as art galleries and antiques shops to explore. The area also has an abundance of festivals, including two in April: The Highland Lakes Bluebonnet Trail and the Old Time Fiddlers' Fest, which is held on the second Saturday. The Llano County Rodeo and Parade is held the first weekend in June, and The Highland Lakes Arts and Crafts Trail takes place the last two weekends in October and the first weekend in November. That first weekend in November also brings Old Boom Days in Llano, with arts, crafts, barbecue cookoffs, and Western dances. The Friday after Thanksgiving, Santa arrives for the lighting of the downtown Christmas lights.

Getting There: The Highland Lakes are about 90 miles north of San Antonio—a two-hour drive via Highway 281.

This regal red-brick edifice with ornate checkerboard-style marble trim is the only two-story building on Llano's main street. Built in a classic Italian Renaissance style, The Badu House was originally the First National Bank of Llano, built in 1891 by Francis Fisher, who contracted to build the structure within forty-five days or else pay a penalty. Records do not show if Fisher met his deadline, but his workmanship is flawless.

After Llano's economy fell in 1898, the bank building was auctioned off, and Professor N. J. Badu, a mineralogist from Nancy, France, bought it as his home. While teaching in Paris, Texas, the brilliant and well-educated Badu met and married Charlie Neal. They moved to Llano, where he managed the Algona Hotel, and later the Driskell in Austin, when he wasn't traveling the countryside promoting the minerals of the area. One of his discoveries in Llano was llanite, a rare type of brown granite with sky-blue crystal and rusty pink feldspar found only in Llano County.

The Badus lived upstairs where they entertained often; the first floor was used for offices and even became a bank again for a while. In 1980 the Badu descendants sold the house to Ann and Earl Ruff, who completely restored the old building, adding modern conveniences like central heating, air-conditioning, and plumbing. In 1985 the present owners, Lance and Kathy Moran, bought the inn and its contents, and have changed little. Many of the elegant touches are original, including the sweeping marble staircase that is now the main entrance, the hand-carved door handles and knobs, the wood floors, and the sliding wooden shutters.

The first-floor dining room is decorated with Victorian pieces and hand-printed cloth wallpaper. There is even a portrait of the professor over the mantle. A complimentary Continental breakfast is served here, and the restaurant, which serves mostly country-style steak and chicken, is open for lunch and dinner.

There is stained glass in the entry, and the chandelier at the top of the stairs was ordered from the Sears catalog in 1901. To the left of the marble staircase is the Llanite Club, so named because its bar top is supposedly the largest piece of polished llanite in the world. Hotel guests are automatically members of the club. Off the bar is a wooden deck and a beer garden.

The seven guest rooms are all on the second floor. Oak panels that once divided the offices of the lawyers and bank vice presidents now separate the rooms, which are decorated with Victorian wallpaper and antiques. The Aberdeen Room, for example, is done in Eastlake pieces with crocheted doilies on the chairs and hand-embroidered dresser scarves and pillowcases. A lace dust ruffle encircles the bed, and the lampshades are made from dresses of the period.

THE BADU HOUSE

601 Bessemer, Box 745,
Llano, Texas 78643

Telephone: (915) 247-4304

Accommodations: seven rooms with twin or double beds; private and shared baths with tub/shower; no telephones; no television.

Rates: moderate, Continental breakfast included. Restaurant open for lunch and dinner, closed Sunday and Monday. Children over thirteen welcome. No pets.

Cards: MC, V

Texas Medallion, National Register. Open all year.

The Badu House

The Tillie Badu Room is a bright corner room with lace curtains and a floral carpet. The Charlie Neal Room has a white wicker bed and shutters instead of curtains. The Professor and Study rooms share the front of the hotel, and can be rented as a suite with a private bath, or as two rooms with shared bath. The baths are small, but each has a claw-foot tub, pedestal washbasin, and pull-chain toilet.

Llano, a typical small town, has become a weekend getaway spot for city residents. The Llano River is two blocks away, and a walking tour of the town is available from the Chamber of Commerce.

Getting There: From San Antonio, take Highway 281 north to the junction of Highway 71. Go west into Llano via Highway 16, which is also Bessemer Street. The inn is two blocks north of the bridge on the left side of the street.

Most innkeepers name their inns after the original owners or the family who lived there the longest. The Harlyn House uses a different approach. Its name is an acronym for Harold and Marilyn Oseen, the inn's present owners, who moved to Marble Falls from Canada in 1981. The narrow little house is painted blue with white trim and set in a yard landscaped with gravel and shrubs.

It was built around 1908 by Nathan Galloway, who owned the general store just down the street. He sold the house in 1944, and it was subsequently rented out as offices. When the Oseens purchased the house, they restored it and furnished it with a combination of family pieces and antiques picked up at auctions.

Although the house is quite small, there are five guest rooms: one on the first floor, two doubles and a small single on the second, and a large third-floor suite.

The Blue Room has a four-poster headboard, lace curtains, and a built-in vanity. The Pink Room, with its bay window, has a full four-poster with a pink quilted coverlet, complemented by a mirrored dresser and a small corner table with a ruffled skirt. The tiny single, done in cheerful pinks and lavenders, is usually rented to families traveling with a child.

The large, dormered attic, now called the Loft, contains a double bed and two singles. The wooden floors are covered with Oriental carpets, and there is a stained-glass window. The sitting area in the private hallway is filled with plants, and in the corner is a tiny bath.

Marilyn provides a full breakfast consisting of sausage, eggs, waffles, breakfast casseroles, and homemade muffins. One of her specialties is an omelet with sour cream, cheese, and picante sauce. Guests are served in the dining room.

HARLYN HOUSE BED AND BREAKFAST

508 Main Street,
Marble Falls, Texas 78654

Telephone: (512) 693-7651

Accommodations: five rooms with twin, double, or queen-size beds; shared and private baths with tub, shower, or tub/shower; no telephones; one television.

Rates: inexpensive, full breakfast included. Well-behaved children welcome. No pets.

No credit cards.

Open all year.

Marble Falls is a small town in the Highland Lakes area of the Texas Hill Country. Each spring the countryside is covered with Indian paintbrush and bluebonnets. Summer is the peak season here, and many of the Oseen's guests come to get away from the heat of San Antonio, just ninety minutes south. Besides fishing, boating, and water skiing on the many lakes in the area, attractions include Enchanted Rock, Longhorn Caverns, and the Vanishing Texas River Cruise.

Getting There: Take Highway 281 from San Antonio to Marble Falls. Go left on Fourth one block to Main and turn right; the inn is on the left. Pickup available from municipal airport at Horseshoe Bay.

Situated halfway between Waco and Austin, the small town of Salado is steeped in history. It was settled in the 1830s, mostly by Scots, on a Mexican land grant obtained by Stephen F. Austin. A college was founded here in 1860, and the town prospered as a well-known stop on the Chisholm Trail; General Custer passed through, Sam Houston made a speech here, and the James boys hid out in a nearby cave. Then the railroad passed it by and the town went into decline.

Salado is still a quiet town, just off the interstate. The blue Colonial house with white two-story columns that is now The Inn at Salado was built in 1873 by the Orgain family. For a while it was used as a boardinghouse for families and students at Salado College. Later, three generations of the Allamon family owned the house, and during that time it was used as a telephone exchange. Mr. Allamon also sold honey from his backyard.

Now owned by innkeepers Barry and Cathy Sands, the inn, on the corner of Pace Park, is just a stone's throw from the Salado (salty) Creek for which the town was named. It is also within walking distance of shops, galleries, and restaurants.

The rooms and suites are all named for people who lived in or visited the town. The Levi Tenney Room, done in peach and white with a simple four-poster and a white chenille spread, was named for the local Presbyterian minister who served as the first president of Salado College.

The Rev. George Washington Baines Room (named for the grandfather of Lyndon Baines Johnson) has a historic bed that Jim Hogg slept in before he was elected governor of Texas. The bed came from a boardinghouse near the University of Texas at Austin, and has a carved headboard and a white crocheted coverlet. These two downstairs rooms share a bath with a footed tub.

The General Custer Suite, off the kitchen, has a large sitting room and opens onto the tree-shaded backyard. The room is furnished with unpainted pieces and

THE INN AT SALADO

North Main at Pace Park, Salado, Texas 76571

Telephone: (817) 947-8200

Accommodations: five rooms with double or king-size beds; private and shared baths with tub or tub/shower; no telephones; television available.

Rates: inexpensive to expensive, full breakfast included. Children over ten welcome. No pets.

Cards: MC, V

No smoking inside the inn. Open all year.

decorated with touches like an old Underwood typewriter. Upstairs are two very large suites. The A. J. Rose Suite has a signature quilt over the bed and a sitting room with a comfortable couch. The private bath has just a shower. The Wilborn Barton Suite is named for a Civil War doctor who lived just down the street and entertained both General Custer and Sam Houston. This suite has two rooms, including a sitting area by the fire with overstuffed couches, a wicker table, and a leather wing chair. It has a private bath down the hall.

Special pieces in the inn include a pine farm table handmade in Burton, Texas, an antique bed handmade by Barry's grandfather, and various pieces accumulated during the Sands' eighteen years of antiques collecting.

The dining room–parlor is filled with country American antiques and Oriental carpets. There is an old stereoscope on a school desk, and a fireplace to warm your feet on cool mornings. A full breakfast is served informally in the dining room or on the tree-shaded patio. The menu usually includes quiche, sausage or ham, pastries, juice, coffee, and fresh fruit.

There are several charming shops within walking distance, a tea room next door for lunch, and a romantic dinner spot just down the street. Several of the historic sites and homes in the area are marked and you can rent taped driving tours of the area. The first weekend in December there is a historic homes tour.

Getting There: Take Interstate 35 north from Austin and exit on Stage Coach Road. Turn right at stop sign, go one block to Main, and turn left. The inn is on your immediate right.

Although just east of the university town of Georgetown, this Texas farmhouse sits in a three-acre pastoral setting. You can hear birds and crickets, and, on hot summer days, sit on the wraparound porch to catch the cooling breeze. The house was built by Jesse Cooper around 1911, perhaps as a wedding present for his bride, Sarah Wilbarger Cooper. For years they filled the house with visitors and parties. Not far from the front porch was a round rock, as flat and large as a patio. Here the ladies would talk and quilt while the men sat on the porch and drank Lone Star beer.

Jesse and his wife lived in the house until his death in 1944, when it passed to his son, who sold it three years later. Sometime in the 1960s an addition that included a kitchen, den, and bath was made at the back.

The present owners, Carol Gafford and Patty Thomas, purchased the house in December of 1985. Already partners in a graphic-art business, the two women

LONE STAR INN OF TEXAS BED AND BREAKFAST

Route 3, Box 1895, Georgetown, Texas 78626

Telephone: (512) 863-7527

Accommodations: four rooms with double beds; private and shared baths with tub or shower; no telephones; television in parlor.

Rates: inexpensive to moderate, full breakfast included. Children over twelve welcome. No pets.

No credit cards.

No smoking inside the inn. Open all year.

Lone Star Inn of Texas Bed and Breakfast

completely restored the interior with such authenticity that one of the Coopers' granddaughters said she felt she'd come home when she saw it.

The hardwood floors were sanded and polished. All the wainscoting was stripped, restained, and varnished. New paint or paper was added to the walls before the rooms were filled with antiques.

The inn was opened in April of 1986. The living room boasts a grand piano, a fireplace, and comfortable furniture from the 1920s. Scattered about are small tables where the hearty breakfast is served. This might include such things as biscuits, eggs, bacon, sausage, pancakes, stuffed french toast, or a breakfast burrito; guests are asked to make their requests the night before. The innkeeper will also prepare lunch or dinner with two days' notice. In the evenings, Carol and Patty offer coffee and dessert, usually an old-fashioned pie such as lemon chess, buttermilk, or chocolate meringue.

The four bedrooms, which open off the upstairs landing, are named for Texas rivers. The largest is San Gabriel, the original master suite. This sunny front room is filled with turn-of-the-century oak pieces that came from the owners' homes. Set against walls covered in taffeta moire is a carved-oak bed with lace coverlet and a velvet settee. The fireplace, which is no longer used, adds a decorative touch with its peach tile. The floors are hardwood, and the his-and-hers closets have the original mirrors. The San Gabriel is one of two rooms that offer a private bath; it has a shower and pedestal sink.

Rio Grande, as its name might imply, is more Southwestern. The walls are painted green with white trim, the hardwood floor is covered with an elk-skin rug, and the bed has a woven coverlet. This room, too, has a private bath with shower only and an antique lavatory in the room.

Guadalupe is done in cool blue and white with an antique iron bed, a small oak desk, and a wicker rocker. Brazos is quite small and often used for a third person traveling with a couple. It is bright and cheerful with its flowered wallpaper and green wooden four-poster. Guadalupe and Brazos share the hall bath, which contains the original six-foot iron tub.

All rooms have a view of the surrounding land covered in oaks and elms. Rabbits and squirrels can be spotted from the porch, as can the occasional roadrunner.

The entire inn may be rented for special parties, business meetings, or reunions. Just behind the inn is the Inn Shoppe, filled with small antiques and collectibles and a line of handmade crafts.

Located just north of Austin, Georgetown is the premier Main Street City in Texas, having revitalized much of its historic downtown with government funds. It is also the home of Southwestern University, the state's oldest institution of higher learning. The main square in downtown Georgetown has been placed on the National Register of Historic Places, and the forty-five restored buildings are fine examples of Victorian commercial architecture.

There is swimming, picnicking, and hiking along Lake Georgetown, and the town hosts various festivals throughout the year, such as Chisholm Trail Days, Octoberfest, Christmas Stroll, and the Sheriff's Posse Rodeo.

Getting There: From Interstate 35, take Highway 29 east 2.7 miles past Southwestern University. Just after the Catholic church, turn left onto Wilbarger Point. You'll see a small sign for the inn, which is another quarter mile down on the left. Transportation available from municipal airport in Georgetown.

Rejina House Southard has a large world map in her study with red pins showing where her guests live. As one might expect, many Texas cities are represented, but so are cities in South America, Europe, the U.S.S.R., China, New Zealand, and India. Many of her international guests are professors who come to the University of Texas to teach or to do research. Others come solely for the pleasure of staying at the inn.

Southard-House is located in a quiet residential neighborhood within walking distance of several excellent restaurants and just nine blocks from Sixth Street, Austin's answer to Bourbon Street. A renovated nineteenth-century business district, Sixth Street is the place to shop by day; at night live music fills the air.

The inn was built as a one-story bungalow in 1890. About 1910, the owners raised the house and constructed a new first floor underneath. The spring under the basement once furnished the whole neighborhood with water.

Guests are greeted in the plant-filled lobby, with its beautiful wood floors, tall windows, and white wicker furniture upholstered in a blue-and-white pattern that matches the wallpaper. The five bedrooms on the second floor are furnished with antiques, collected from shops and auctions, that recreate the aura of a nineteenth-century manor house. Most rooms have white-iron and brass beds, lace curtains, and embroidered cutwork bedspreads and pillowcases imported from China. The walls are papered with pastel prints, and the art is mostly original.

Little brass signs designate the various rooms. Treaty Oaks, named for the traditional ancient site for signing peace treaties, can be either a single room or a two-room suite with sitting area. There is a marble-topped dresser and a sofa bed in the sitting room, along with a fireplace.

SOUTHARD-HOUSE

908 Blanco,
Austin, Texas 78703

Telephone: (512) 474-4731

Accommodations: five rooms with double or queen-size beds; private baths with shower or tub/shower; telephone in sitting room; television available on request.

Rates: moderate to expensive, Continental breakfast on weekdays, full breakfast on weekends included. Children over twelve welcome. No pets.

Cards: AE, MC, V

No smoking in the inn. Open all year.

Rolling Stone was named after the weekly published by O. Henry during the decade he lived in Austin at the end of the last century. Lady Esther was named for Esther Coffey, who lived in the house for fifty years. The Tickanwatic commemorates an early tribe of Indians who lived in the area. The Moonlight Room, originally meant to be a tower room, is named for the 165-foot mercury-vapor lamps that have shed silvery "moonlight" over Austin since 1894. (Of the original thirty-one lamp towers, twenty-one remain.) All the rooms have private baths, some with claw-foot tubs and others with showers only. The sitting room on the first floor has a television and dozens of magazines for browsing.

Coffee is ready by six-thirty in the morning for early risers, and a gourmet breakfast is served later in the dining room (Continental on weekdays, full on weekends). By candlelight, and beside a roaring fire on chilly mornings, Rejina serves Mexican eggs, cinnamon rolls, eggs Benedict or Belgian waffles, along with the morning paper.

The dining room has mauve walls, white lace curtains, and a cutwork tablecloth similar to the bedspreads. The wooden chandelier is made from carved dragons that hold the lightbulbs in their mouths. Just outside the dining room is a gazebo where guests often take their breakfast on summer mornings.

In 1838 Mirabeau Lamar, vice president of the Republic of Texas, camped near the present site of Austin on the edge of the Colorado River, and was so impressed with the location that he suggested it as the permanent capital. The favorable elevation of the area, which kept it free of bayou fevers, outweighed the dangers of being on the edge of the frontier. The town was named in honor of Stephen F. Austin, colonizer of the first American settlement in Texas, and is still the state capital.

In the early 1970s, country musicians and bands began moving to Austin, making it a second Nashville and the birthplace of progressive country music. Other local attractions include the O. Henry Museum with many of the author's personal effects, and the Governor's Mansion, where tours are offered.

For a little old-fashioned fun, Austin has one of the largest "swimmin' holes" in the country, located on the Colorado River, which flows through the city. Lake Austin offers boating, fishing, and swimming. The Bluebonnet Trail takes place in April, when the countryside turns a spectacular blue. The Pecan Street Festival is held twice a year, in May and September, and the Governor's Cup Sailing Regatta is held in July.

Getting There: Take the Sixth Street exit off Interstate 35 and go west past the downtown area. Continue on Sixth Street three blocks past Lamar to Blanco and turn right. The inn is the large white Victorian three blocks down on the left. Transportation available from Austin airport.

The big yellow house belonging to Charles and Marilyn Whites is on the National Register and sports a Texas Medallion. Since the Whites' work in Austin (Charles with the IRS and Marilyn in the chemistry department at the University of Texas), the inn is open only on Friday and Saturday nights as a weekend getaway. A local lumberyard owner named Pfeiffer built the Carpenter Gothic house of pine and cypress in 1901, and it still retains the original ornate trim, wavy glass windows, transoms, and high ceilings.

The inn is filled with antiques collected over the years, augmented with modern pieces and reproduction furniture. Other collections also fill the house—dolls, toys, pewter, and quilts—giving the wide platforms along the staircase the air of an antiques shop display. The parlor is a formal room with Victorian chairs, settees, and knickknacks everywhere. Glass instruments from the chemistry department are used as vases and domes, or set out like pieces of art. The downstairs sitting room, done in Early American pine, is less formal.

The three guest rooms are on the second floor, sharing one large bath with swagged curtains over the tub and stacks of fluffy towels. All the quilts are handmade, and when guests arrive there are fresh flowers in their rooms. Coffee is served on trays on the upstairs landing early in the morning, and a full breakfast is served later in the formal dining room.

The largest room is called Kathy's. The bed, set under the eaves, has swagged drapes to emulate a half-tester. There is a small writing desk in the window nook, and a sitting area under the eaves against the opposite wall. Charlie's Room, also set under the eaves, is a cozy spot with twin beds, log-cabin quilts, a Shaker pegboard to hang clothes on, and an old rocker by the dormer window. Outside the room is a small hallway and another display of collectibles, this one focused on an old steamer trunk overflowing with antique clothes.

The smallest room, Grandma's, has an old iron double bed with a bright, rose-colored chintz spread and, like the other rooms, a stained-glass window. There is plenty of reading material in the house, and in the summer Marilyn serves refreshments on the porch. There are wicker chairs on the side porch and a swing under the pecan trees—special places to relax and unwind from hectic city life. Many of the guests come from Dallas, San Antonio, and Austin to do just that.

Bastrop was Stephen Austin's third major colony in Texas. As grumblings of unrest grew, the town became a hotbed of rebellion against the Mexican government. Three of its citizens signed the Texas Declaration of Independence, eleven died at the Alamo, and sixty fought at San Jacinto.

PFEIFFER HOUSE

1802 Main Street,
Bastrop, Texas 78602

Telephone: (512) 321-2100

Accommodations: three rooms with twin or double beds; shared bath with tub/shower; no telephones; no television.

Rates: moderate, full breakfast included. No children. No pets.

No credit cards.

No smoking in rooms. Texas Medallion, National Register. Open Friday and Saturday only.

Pfeiffer House

Today, 131 buildings and sites in this small community, located 45 minutes from Austin, are on the National Register of Historic Places. The buildings, dating from the mid-nineteenth to early twentieth centuries, represent a cross-section of architectural styles—from pioneer log houses to antebellum Greek Revival homes to gingerbread Victorians.

There are two golf courses in the area. One of Bastrop's most famous landmarks is the Lost Pines, a stand of Eastern pine trees. The 1889 Opera House has been restored, and melodramas are performed there June through August. The Chamber of Commerce provides both walking and driving tours, and private homes are open during Historic Tours in June and December.

Getting There: From Austin take Highway 71 into Bastrop. At the first flashing red light turn left and go over the bridge. Turn left again at the next light onto Main Street and go several blocks. The house is on the left.

Set back from the highway by a swath of green, Aquarena Springs Inn sits on the edge of crystal-blue Spring Lake, looking like a cross between a white barge and a Mediterranean villa. Broad steps lead down to the water's edge, and blue iron railings trim the balconies of the two-story stucco building.

Surrounded by cypress trees, the lake is home to scores of ducks and geese. During the day, glass-bottom boats and swans glide past. Across the lake, at the end of a small peninsula, is the mini–amusement park that had its start in the 1950s. Here, a Western village sits at the edge of the tree-lined water. The underwater stage for the regularly scheduled shows and the dock for the glass-bottom boats are also clustered at this end of the small lake. Since there is no restaurant at the inn (although a Continental breakfast is served to guests), everyone must cross the lake to dine in the park's restaurant or at any of the dozens of restaurants near the University, just a few blocks away.

The lake, actually part of the San Marcos River, is kept at a constant temperature of 71° F by underwater springs formed by the Balcones Fault. Discovered by Spanish explorers, the springs were a major stop on the Old San Antonio Road. Much later, in 1929, the inn opened as a spa called the Spring Lake Inn. A golf course was added, then the glass-bottom boats, and eventually the underwater show. During the 1940s the complex was turned into a sanitarium, which closed after World War II. The place then became a school for exceptional children. In the late 1950s Aquarena Springs was again a hotel. The inn was remodeled and reopened in 1962.

AQUARENA SPRINGS INN

One Aquarena Springs Drive, San Marcos, Texas 78666

Telephone: (512) 396-8900

Accommodations: twenty-five rooms with double beds, one with king-size bed; private baths with tub/shower; telephones; television.

Rates: moderate, Continental breakfast included. Children welcome. No pets.

Cards: AE, CB, DC, MC, V

Open all year.

The lobby is light, with large windows and mirrors, antique furniture, and Oriental carpets on the swirl-patterned brick floor. From the hallway, another set of large windows opens onto the moss-covered rocks against which the hotel is built. Considering the setting and the history of the building, it is a little disappointing to find that the rooms resemble those in any comfortable motel, with modern furniture and color televisions. A few even have kitchenettes.

The nineteen rooms overlooking the lagoon each have their own balconies. The other six rooms are at the back of the hotel, and their windows open onto a wall of natural rock, dripping with moisture and plants, which gives them an almost cavelike atmosphere. Guests have access to these hanging gardens from the second-floor hall. A nature walk meanders through the woods, and trails lead to an artisans' studio where you can watch glass blowers, the historic Burleson Home (an old log cabin), the Spanish mission, and the gristmill. Although it's an easy walk around the lake, a bell at the ferry landing will summon a boat to take you across, or you may take the Swiss sky ride from one side to the other. Although the lake is no longer used for swimming, it is still the focal point of the inn. Glass-bottom boats depart on a regular schedule for a tour of the lake and a glimpse of the underwater archaeological site where anthropologists uncovered remains of Clovis Man, who lived in this region over twelve thousand years ago.

Although Aquarena Springs is the main tourist attraction in San Marcos, guests come to the inn to relax, to walk in the gardens, to lounge by the Olympic-size pool, to play a few holes of golf, or just to watch the ducks on the lake.

Other local attractions include Belvin Street Historic District, a superb example of nineteenth-century architecture. Although the houses are all privately owned, many are open to the public during the Tours of Distinction in May. The San Marcos River Walkway takes visitors through three of the city's parks along the river, and at Wonder World visitors are invited to see one of the largest earthquake-formed caves in the United States. In September is the annual Chilympiad, the official state championship chili cookoff, and in May, Texans celebrate their Mexican heritage with Cinco de Mayo.

Getting There: Take Interstate 35 north from San Antonio. Take exit 206 in San Marcos and turn left at the stoplight. Go one mile, passing the railroad tracks, to the inn's entrance on the right.

NEW BRAUNFELS

The German immigrants who came to the springs at the headwaters of the Comal River hadn't planned to settle there. They were headed farther west toward the Medina River, but the negotiations for land there didn't work out, and in the spring of 1845 an agreement was made for acquisition of land at the confluence of the Comal and Guadalupe rivers.

The settlers named their town New Braunfels after the home of their leader, Prince Carl of Solms-Braunfels. As commissioner-general for the Adelsverein (Association of Noblemen), he was responsible for making all the arrangements for the new colony. The new inhabitants arrived by ox cart on Good Friday, 1845, and found the area sparsely populated except for the Indians. The town prospered and was for a while one of the largest in Texas.

Prince Carl planned to build a castle for his fiancée, Lady Sophia, Princess of Salm-Salm, on a hill overlooking the city. But she refused to come to Texas, and Prince Carl eventually returned to Germany. Though the castle was never built, the hill is still called Sophienburg.

New Braunfels is a beautiful city. The Comal River, which flows only three and a half miles before becoming part of the Guadalupe, is unique: It is the only river in the world that begins and ends within the same city. Many of the historic buildings have been restored, and the town square, as the Prince intended, is still the center of local activity. A self-guided walking tour of the town is available.

New Braunfels' main attractions, however, are its antiques shops; several times a year, antiques dealers from all over the country present shows. In the fall, the town celebrates Wurstfest with ten days of dancing, sausage eating, and beer drinking. Early fall is also time for the Comal County Fair.

Landa Park, a series of islands and peninsulas created by the meandering Comal River, is shaded by ancient oaks and offers innertubing and paddle boating, two swimming pools, an eighteen-hole golf course, and fireworks on the Fourth of July. John Newcombe's Tennis Ranch is just outside the city.

Canyon Lake (twelve miles away by the River Road, following the scenic Guadalupe River) offers canoeing, rafting, sailing, and ninety-five miles of shoreline. Visitors can view exotic African and Asian animals at Natural Bridge Wildlife Park, or take a tour through the caverns.

Getting There: New Braunfels is just north of San Antonio on Interstate 35.

The hotel is a gracious throwback to an elegant time of courtly gentlemen and beautiful ladies. Emilie Eggeling, an early settler of New Braunfels, had faith that the city would grow and prosper. In 1899 she hired German craftsmen to build the hotel to last, using native materials. (The cypress was locally milled, and the beige brick was handmade on the banks of the Guadalupe River and hauled to the site in horse-drawn wagons.) Mrs. Eggeling ran the hotel for twenty-six years and her daughters carried on the tradition until 1952.

Originally named for the Comal River, the hotel now bears the name of the city's founder, Prince Carl Solms-Braunfels. The prince would have felt at home here. Beyond the ten-foot etched-glass doors, one hears the soft strains of classical music. The parlor is the epitome of Victorian grandeur, adorned with needlepoint, Oriental carpets, and a selection of art magazines. In the evening, guests gather under a portrait of the prince for coffee and brandy from the cellar restaurant.

Betty Mitchell and Marge Crumbaker bought the empty hotel in 1977 and refurnished it. All the original bronze fittings from Europe were intact and much of the wallpaper from the 1950s remains in good condition. The pictures that now hang on the walls were found stashed in closets.

There are three suites on the first floor: the Carl, the Sophie (Prince Solms' betrothed), and the Lahn (named for the river near the prince's German home). Each suite has a bedroom and a sitting room, with windows nearly as tall as the fourteen-foot ceilings. The suites also have small refrigerators.

Eight smaller rooms occupy the second floor, and are named primarily for their wallpaper patterns. These rooms have louvered "privacy doors" set in the main doors to let the air circulate on hot days. All rooms have private baths stocked with Yardley soaps; two have footed tubs.

The Summer House is a corner room done in lavender and lace, with a thirteen-foot green bead-board ceiling. The pink-and-red Rose Room is very feminine, too, with roses on the wallpaper, lace curtains, and a mirrored armoire. The cozy Library is one of the more masculine rooms, with a king-size bed set in front of a wall of books, and in the corner a table and two velvet-covered chairs; the bath is rather tiny. Huntsman is another masculine-style room with wallpaper depicting hunting scenes, a brown-and-green color scheme, and a large wing chair. Magnolia, done in bold black and white with touches of green, has a brass and black-iron bedstead. Penelope is a corner room with twin carved-maple beds, Song Bird has a tiny alcove with tables and chairs, and Peony has a carved bed.

Arriving guests are welcomed with a bowl of fruit in their rooms. Breakfast is served buffet style in the upstairs hall, or delivered on tea carts to guests staying in

PRINCE SOLMS INN

295 East San Antonio,
New Braunfels, Texas 78130

Telephone: (512) 625-9169

Accommodations: eleven rooms with twin, double, or king-size beds; private baths with shower or tub/shower; no telephones; no television.

Rates: moderate to very expensive, Continental breakfast included. Wolfgang's Keller open for dinner Tuesday through Sunday. Children discouraged. No pets.

Cards: MC, V

Meeting facilities. National Register. Open all year.

Prince Solms Inn

the suites. The Continental breakfast includes a choice of croissants, muffins, or pastries from a local German bakery.

The green-and-pink theme of the hotel is carried out in Wolfgang's Keller. Located in the cellar (where Mrs. Eggeling grew mushrooms to sell from her fringed surrey), this dark, intimate restaurant is filled with antiques and Old World charm. The Continental cuisine features veal parmigiana or marsala, linguini with shrimp and clam sauce, steak, or a German country plate. The adjacent bar is small and filled with Victorian sofas and chairs where patrons sip champagne or mixed drinks. After dinner Lynn Peters entertains at the piano.

Behind the hotel, a marvelous enclosed garden is also a popular spot for drinks, as well as private parties. Brick walkways wind among the wrought-iron tables and chairs, Chinese lanterns hang from the trees, and there is even a covered patio with a corner fireplace for chilly evenings.

Close to both San Antonio and Austin, Prince Solms Inn is an ideal romantic getaway, and many celebrities have found it so; state senators, movie stars, and sports figures are among the famous visitors.

Getting There: Take McQueeny Exit off Interstate 35 at New Braunfels. Go under the freeway to the traffic circle and take the first right which is East San Antonio. The inn is on the left. Transportation available from New Braunfels municipal airport with advance notice.

The Hotel Faust was considered the finest hostelry in Texas when it opened in 1929. Extravagantly appointed with custom-designed ornamental stonework on the facade, it had sixty-three rooms, each with a closet, a French telephone, and a private bath—luxuries in those days. The New Braunfels Herald of October 18, 1929, stated: "The lobby is floored with a beautiful Spanish tile in a design and color especially selected for this building. All of the walls are plastered and decorated to imitate the real Travertine stone from Italy. Columns and pilasters have unusually decorative caps, and the soffits of all the main beams are decorated in stencil work, while the ceiling itself is stippled out in a delicate tint."

Then called the Travelers Hotel, it quickly became a fashionable overnight stop and a favorite dining spot for local citizens. Among the frequent guests were salesmen who set up their wares in their rooms. When the Depression hit, the financially troubled hotel was taken over by Walter Faust, a bank president and one of New Braunfels' most prosperous citizens. In 1936, a few years after Faust's death, the Travelers Hotel was renamed in his honor.

HOTEL FAUST

240 South Seguin,
New Braunfels, Texas 78130

Telephone: (512) 625-7791

Accommodations: sixty-two rooms with double or king-size beds; private baths with shower or tub/shower; telephones; television.

Rates: inexpensive, no meals included. Restaurant open for breakfast, lunch, and dinner. Children welcome. No pets.

Cards: AE, CB, DC, MC, V

Wheelchair access. Meeting facilities. Texas Medallion, National Register. Open all year.

During World War II, the Faust earned the nickname "Honeymoon Hotel": Servicemen, on three-day honeymoon passes from military bases around nearby San Antonio, brought their brides to this elegant hotel. The Heritage Room, a private dining area in the hotel, is lined with wedding pictures from this era.

The four-story hotel has been renovated twice since 1977, has been designated a Texas Historic Landmark, and is listed on the National Register. The original mirrored elevator, floored in parquet, whisks guests from the spacious lobby (which looks much as it did in 1929) to the three stories of guest rooms. Each floor has walnut woodwork and its own color scheme. The second floor is done predominantly in rust, the third in blue, and the fourth in emerald green.

Unlike many renovated hotels, the rooms have not been enlarged. In fact, some of the sixty-one rooms are quite small, and some of the bathrooms are positively tiny, but many of the rooms adjoin to form small suites. A large corner two-room suite with an adjoining third room is often used for receptions.

The decoration is spare. Some of the original furniture remains, augmented by antiques and modern pieces, such as the king-size beds in many of the rooms. Old-fashioned paddle fans stir the air, and a few pictures hang from wires, as they did in the 1920s.

The Faust is still a good place to eat. The lunch menu offers primarily soup, salad, and sandwiches; dinner features steak and seafood.

Getting There: Take the McQueeney exit off Interstate 10 (Seguin Boulevard) and go left (under the freeway). The hotel is on the left just before the traffic circle (Main Square).

Castroville is a quiet village just a few miles outside of San Antonio. Originally an Alsatian community, it boasts many limestone buildings with gabled, wood-shingled roofs, similar to farmhouses built in the Alsace-Lorraine region of Europe in the mid-1800s. The town is proud of its heritage; many of the older townspeople still speak a dialect of Alsatian, and a local group performs traditional dances of the region in folk costume.

The genesis of the Landmark Inn, however, dates back to an Irish immigrant, John Vance, who bought a one-story building on the Old San Antonio Highway just a few yards from where it crossed the Medina River. Though Castroville today is only thirty minutes from the Alamo, in the 1850s it was a day's journey, making the town a good place for an overnight stop.

Vance opened a general store. Because of the heavy traffic, he soon added a second story and rented out rooms to travelers as well. Later he added the

LANDMARK INN

Highway 90, Box 577,
Castroville, Texas 78009

Telephone: (512) 538-2133

Accommodations: eight rooms with twin or double beds; shared and private baths with shower only; no telephones; no television.

Rates: inexpensive, no meals included. Children welcome. No pets.

No credit cards.

No smoking inside rooms. One room equipped for the handicapped. Texas Medallion, National Register. Open all year.

Landmark Inn

bathhouse, and the Vance Hotel, as it became known, was the only place between San Antonio and Del Rio where a traveler could get a hot bath.

The area prospered. Vance sold his riverfront property to George Haass and Laurent Quintle, who in 1854 built a gristmill so the local farmers no longer had to travel into San Antonio to have their corn ground.

Tradition says that Robert E. Lee, a friend of Vance's, often stayed at the hotel. Another tale tells how the lead lining of the old bathhouse was stripped and melted down for Confederate bullets during the Civil War.

In 1935 Jordan T. Lawler and his sister Ruth purchased the mill, the inn, and the Vance residence and outbuildings. The mill was modernized again, this time bringing Castroville its first electricity. During World War II, the Lawlers reopened the hotel and named it the Landmark Inn, and in 1974 Ruth donated the property and the buildings to the State of Texas. Now run by the State Parks Department, the inn has six rooms in the main building and two more in the bathhouse.

The setting is stunning. There are several whitewashed limestone buildings in the complex. The grounds, partially landscaped and partially left wild and woodsy, follow the curve of the land down to the river. Here the stone mill stands in empty ruins, a testament to a less complicated era. All the rooms but one have views of the back courtyard or the mill, as well as the woods surrounding the river.

The rooms are simply furnished. The wood floors are either carpeted or have area rugs, and the walls are painted in white or soft pastels. The furniture is mostly old rather than antique, as is appropriate in a country hotel. There are four-posters or iron beds, armoires, quilts, and wicker chairs in the rooms. Some of the pieces, like the Morris chair and the music stand in the Robert E. Lee Room, were donated by Ruth Lawler, who, now in her eighties, still lives in the Vance home.

The old bathhouse rooms have low ceilings and short doors; even a person of average height must duck to enter the upstairs room. It has a rough wood-beam ceiling, braided rugs, and simple country furniture set against the whitewashed walls.

The rooms are not air conditioned, but the eighteen-inch-thick limestone walls keep them cool even on the hottest days, and there are dozens of shade trees.

There are numerous restaurants in town, and an abundance of Alsatian bakeries. Guests often bring back pastries and eat them on the hotel's balcony. Guests may also bring liquor to drink in the privacy of their rooms, but they must remember that this is a state park and public consumption of alcohol is not allowed.

The lobby closes at six o'clock and late arrivals must call before then to find out where their keys will be left.

Getting There: Take Highway 90 from San Antonio to Castroville. At the second traffic light, turn left into the inn's parking lot.

Reiffert-Mugge Inn is one of the loveliest in Texas. Part of its charm is that so much is original, from the century-old wallpaper in the formal rooms downstairs to the collection of toys belonging to the son of one of the early inhabitants. And it also has a most unusual history.

Emil Reiffert was a Confederate veteran, president of H. Runge and Company (the first chartered bank in Texas), and a respected citizen of the German settlement of Indianola in the mid-nineteenth century. After the Civil War, Indianola, a thriving seaport near Matagorda Island southeast of Cuero, became a wealthy, cosmopolitan community.

Unfortunately, the city was also right in the path of frequent Gulf Coast hurricanes. When the first disastrous storm hit the town in 1875, Reiffert's home was one of the few buildings spared. Others were not so fortunate. Scores of families dismantled their houses, loaded them on flatcars, and had them hauled, board by board, to Cuero, where they were reassembled. Reiffert was one of the few who chose to stay and help rebuild the town.

Eleven years later, the port city was again devastated by a hurricane. Old diaries tell how a hundred people took refuge on the second floor of the Reiffert house. Reiffert's daughter was tied to her mother to keep them together, and his sons were stationed with knives at the top of the stairs to cut off the heads of snakes seeking dry land. During the night, the refugees could hear the piano hitting the ceiling as it floated on the flood waters below. Later, fire destroyed most of what was left of the town. Yet, again, Reiffert's home survived.

The day after the storm, Emil Reiffert bought land in Cuero, dismantled his house, and reassembled it there. When his daughter Hilda married, her husband Fred Mugge moved in with his in-laws and the Mugge descendants lived in the house until the 1950s.

Thus it was by chance that Cuero, a rough-and-tumble cow town near the head of the Chisholm Trail, inherited many wealthy families and their beautiful homes. Cuero is still a small town with a population of only 7,000, yet 1,174 of its buildings are over fifty years old, many of them originally built in Indianola.

The Reiffert-Mugge house is now owned by Gil and Lisa Becker. The original cypress siding was long ago stuccoed over and is painted a soft brown. The extensive grounds are surrounded by an iron fence and shaded by live oaks.

The bare wood floors show where the house was added onto after it was moved: The heart of pine in the dining room is original, the red pine in the hallway was added in 1887. The wallpaper in the parlor and living rooms was also hung at this time, and though over a century old, it is in excellent condition.

REIFFERT-MUGGE INN

304 West Prairie,
Cuero, Texas 77954

Telephone: (512) 275-2626

Accommodations: five rooms and one cottage with twin, double, queen-, or king-size beds; private baths (some down the hall) with shower or tub/shower; telephones available; television on request.

Rates: inexpensive to moderate, full breakfast included. Children over twelve welcome. No pets.

No credit cards.

Facilities for receptions and dinners by reservation. Texas Medallion. Open all year.

Reiffert-Mugge Inn

The Beckers have decorated the house with a few beautiful antique pieces rather than cluttering it with reproductions. Many of the furnishings are from the Reiffert-Mugge family, including most of the lace curtains. In the parlor, a glassed-in lawyer's bookcase is filled with Emil's books, all in German, and an old Victrola in the living room still plays records from the 1920s.

The guest rooms upstairs are named for Reiffert-Mugge family members. Emil's Room has the oldest pieces. The wardrobe is original to the house, but the rice bed (so named for the carvings on the four posts) is a reproduction. Gil's mother's wedding chest, which she brought from Germany, stands at the foot of the bed. Helena's Room, named for Mrs. Reiffert, has a canopy bed, a large armoire, and paintings, photographs, and fixtures that are original to the house. The twin-bedded Nursery displays toys that belonged to the Mugge's son, Freddie Jr. Freddie's Room is decorated in the style of the 1920s and 30s, and Hilda's Room is Art Deco. Reached by going outside onto the second story porch, it is the largest room in the house. The prints on the wall belonged to Hilda's aunt.

The sixth guest room is in the "Radio House," which Fred built when his mother-in-law refused to let him bring a new-fangled instrument called a radio into the house. This cottage, under the spreading live oaks, was just big enough for the radio equipment, a pool table, and a keg of beer. It has been redone in a country style with an iron-and-brass bed, handmade quilts, and arts and crafts on the wall.

Each room has a private bath, though three of them are down the hall. Each hall bath, however, is color coordinated with the appropriate room.

The Beckers serve a full breakfast, often consisting of country brunch pie, baked apples, and Gil's scratch biscuits, as well as homemade jellies.

Every now and then, the Beckers arrange a mystery weekend, usually for groups of four to six couples. Gil wrote the play the guests act out, and he has included most of the town in the search for clues. The mystery weekends are a package deal including two nights lodging, breakfasts, dinners, brandy, and desserts.

Cuero, about two hours south of San Antonio, is in the part of Texas that was intensely involved in the revolution against Mexico. Nearby is Gonzales, where the first shots of revolt were fired, and Goliad, where the Declaration of Texas Independence was signed.

In the fall there are festivals throughout the area, such as the Turkey Fest in October. A walking tour of town is available, and you can rent a tape-recorded guide for a drive around the area. The inn also has bicycles for guests' use.

Getting There: Coming from the north on Highway 183, turn right on Reuss at the first light in town. Reuss becomes Indianola after the curve. Inn is the brown building at the corner of Indianola and Prairie. Transportation available from the municipal airport.

TEXAS COAST

HOUSTON

GALVESTON

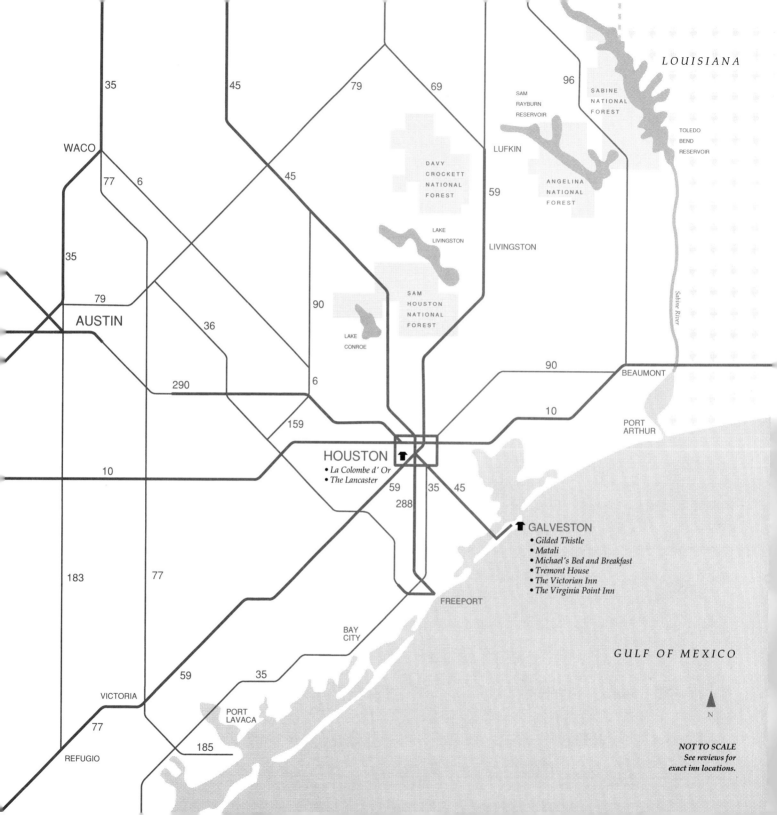

LOUISIANA

35

45

79

69

96   SABINE
NATIONAL
FOREST

SAM
RAYBURN
RESERVOIR

TOLEDO
BEND
RESERVOIR

WACO

77   6

45

DAVY
CROCKETT
NATIONAL
FOREST

LUFKIN

ANGELINA
NATIONAL
FOREST

35

59

LAKE
LIVINGSTON

LIVINGSTON

79

AUSTIN

36

90

SAM
HOUSTON
NATIONAL
FOREST

Sabine River

290

6

LAKE
CONROE

90   BEAUMONT

159

10

PORT
ARTHUR

10

HOUSTON

📍
• *La Colombe d' Or*
• *The Lancaster*

59   35   45

288

📍 GALVESTON

• *Gilded Thistle*
• *Matali*
• *Michael's Bed and Breakfast*
• *Tremont House*
• *The Victorian Inn*
• *The Virginia Point Inn*

183   77

FREEPORT

GULF OF MEXICO

BAY
CITY

▲
N

59   35

VICTORIA

NOT TO SCALE
See reviews for
exact inn locations.

77

PORT
LAVACA

185

REFUGIO

HOUSTON

The Spanish were here by 1524; pirates arrived three centuries later. Stephen Austin colonized the area around 1825, selling land for twelve and a half cents an acre. Yet this part of Texas, now the site of Houston, was still sparsely inhabited swampland in April, 1836, when the deciding battle in the Texas fight for independence took place nearby. General Sam Houston led his small army against the larger Mexican forces under General Santa Anna. The battle, at a place called San Jacinto, lasted only eighteen minutes.

A few months later, two New Yorkers tried to buy a swampy Texas town site called Harrisburg. Unable to make a deal, they found a suitable site a bit farther north and named it for the victorious Sam Houston. The town grew and, for a short time, was even the capital of the new Republic of Texas.

The construction of the Houston Ship Channel in the early part of this century made this inland city, fifty miles from the Gulf, prosper as one of the busiest ports in the nation, outstripping Galveston by the 1920s.

This part of Texas was cotton country until oil was discovered, and it was oil that built the Houston skyline of glass and steel. Although staggering now under the blow of the oil industry's decline, Houston is still a cosmopolitan city, the fourth largest in the United States. It is host to more than fifty foreign consular offices and to the representatives of over six hundred foreign companies.

Houston offers restaurants, art galleries, shops, and nightclubs as well as ballet, grand opera, symphony, live theater, and a year-long calendar of events. In the spring the annual Museum of Natural Science Home Tour and the River Oaks Garden Club's Azalea Trail draw visitors. The Houston Festival takes place in April, ten days of art and culture in the parks and performing arts halls throughout the city. In July, Houston presents a Shakespeare Festival. The fall celebrations are international: the Mexican Fiestas Patrias, the Mediterranean Festival with ethnic foods and crafts, the German Octoberfest, and the Greek Festival. Christmas brings the traditional candlelight tour of historic homes.

Just south of Houston is Clear Lake; in this small community, the past meets the future. Not far from eighth-century Indian burial sites is NASA's Mission Control, located at the Johnson Space Center, as well as its mission simulation and training facility. Just south of Houston, the tallest masonry structure in the world commemorates the battle site at San Jacinto.

Getting There: Houston has two airports: Intercontinental, north of town, and Hobby in the south.

Innkeeper Steven Zimmerman believes three things make life worth living: art, food, and wine. You'll find plenty of all three at La Colombe d'Or. The inn is modeled after the three-star *auberges* in the south of France, noted for their attention to fine food, impeccable service, and elegant surroundings. In fact, the inn's namesake in St. Paul de Vence on the French Riviera is particularly noted for its art collection, acquired over the years from patrons who paid for room and board with their paintings. Today, museums vie over the works of those same patrons: Miró, Chagall, Picasso.

Although tiny (there are only six suites in the hotel), Houston's La Colombe d'Or has gained a reputation for excellence. It has been selected as one of only ten American hotels (and one of only 347 in the world) for membership in the exclusive French-based Relais et Châteaux Association.

The inn's staff of thirty-six all speak both French and English. Guests are welcomed with fresh fruit and Perrier; there are plush robes to wear after bathing, and a Continental breakfast each morning. The inn also offers twenty-four-hour concierge, telex, and secretarial services.

The six suites, filled with antiques, are appropriately named for French painters, and each has its own dining room, some seating as many as eighteen. Renoir has an Asian flair, with an Oriental screen in place of a headboard; its dining room is in an enclosed porch overlooking the front of the inn. Van Gogh is done in bright orange and green with Oriental carpets and two walls of windows. The Penthouse occupies the entire third floor and is virtually one huge area, except for a small wicker-filled sitting room and the bath, complete with whirlpool tub; the bed is hidden behind a large Oriental screen.

The lobby is small and intimate, with Victorian antiques and Oriental carpets on the parquet floors. Here, as throughout the inn, are original paintings and sculptures. Adjacent to the lobby is the bar, with one entire wall covered by a wine rack. There are nooks for sitting and sipping after-dinner brandy, or, if you prefer, you can take your drink into the library, a decidedly masculine room with leather chairs and dark wood.

The restaurant's four small dining rooms occupy most of the ground floor. The main room has a fireplace, and the rose-hued dome room has ornamental plaster work on the walls and ceilings. The garden room is done in greens, and the sun room is a glassed-in porch. On pleasant days, lunch is also served on the front porch.

The restaurant, consistently rated the best in Houston, is something of a European gathering place. One is just as likely to hear a business lunch being conducted in French as in English. The food, mostly French Provençal cuisine, is all

LA COLOMBE D'OR

3410 Montrose Boulevard, Houston, Texas 77006

Telephone: (713) 524-7999

Accommodations: five suites and a penthouse with king-size beds; private baths with tub/shower; private dining room in each suite; telephones; television.

Rates: very expensive, Continental breakfast included. Restaurant open for lunch and dinner Monday through Friday, dinner only on Saturday. Children welcome. No pets.

Cards: AE, CB, DC, MC, V

Meeting facilities. Open all year.

prepared to order. As in the finest restaurants in Europe, there is only one seating for dinner, and guests are expected to wear proper attire. On the menu you'll find everything from Russian caviar to white chocolate mousse.

Although its prices make the restaurant exclusive, it is not snooty. Far from being the place to see and be seen, La Colombe d'Or is a place to relax, have an exceptionally fine meal, and enjoy the extensive offering of wines that Steve personally selects in France twice a year.

The inn was built in 1923 on the outskirts of Houston as the home of Walter Fondren, one of the founders of the company that was to become Exxon. Although Fondren died in 1939, his wife lived in the twenty-one-room house until the mid-1950s, when she turned it over to the Red Cross. Steve and Rebecca Zimmerman purchased the property in 1979. Today, the inn's clientele includes an impressive list of celebrities and many members of the French diplomatic corps.

And although there are only six suites in Houston's La Colombe d'Or, the "seventh" room, as Steven calls it, is a 250-year-old villa for rent in the south of France, overlooking the Mediterranean.

Getting There: Take the Montrose exit off Interstate 45 (Allen Parkway). Turn left and go 3 or 4 miles; the inn will be on your right.

Located in the midst of Civic Center, the Lancaster has come a long way since 1926, when it housed wrestlers from the City Auditorium. After an eight-million-dollar restoration, the hotel now has a clientele primarily of international business people, although it also attracts patrons of the famous Nina Vance Alley Theater and Jones Hall for the Performing Arts, both just across the street.

Since weekends tend to be quiet, the hotel offers several packages to entice guests. The Romantic Weekend includes champagne, chocolates, roses, and a Continental breakfast; optional are theater tickets, dinner for two, or a chauffeur-driven Rolls Royce to pick you up and return you home. The Theater Package includes dinner for two at the Lancaster Grille, a Continental breakfast, and of course theater tickets; if you like, the hotel will arrange a pre-theater reception for your friends in the Presidential Suite.

The multilingual staff provides amenities such as in-house valet service, twenty-four-hour room service, and complimentary limousine service in downtown Houston. The hotel also maintains a membership at the Texas Club, where its guests can enjoy the use of this premier health facility. Turn-down service in the evening includes a bedside glass of brandy.

THE LANCASTER

701 Texas Avenue,
Houston, Texas 77002

Telephone: (713) 228-9500
or (800) 231-0336

Accommodations: eighty-five rooms and eight suites with queen- or king-size beds; private baths with tub and shower; telephones; television.

Rates: very expensive, no meals included. Lancaster Grille open for breakfast, lunch, and dinner. Children welcome. Small pets allowed.

Cards: AE, CB, DC, MC, V

Nonsmoking rooms available. Some rooms equipped for the handicapped. Convention facilities. Texas Medallion. Open all year.

The hotel's original 165 rooms were reduced to 85 rooms and 8 suites during restoration, with no more than 9 rooms on each floor, giving guests both privacy and quiet. A brass and mirrored elevator carries you in style to a foyer on each floor decorated with antiques and fresh flowers.

The guest rooms are all quite large and decorated somewhat alike, with varying color schemes of white, yellow, green, or rose. All are richly appointed with dark wood, bright English chintz, and custom-made furniture. Each room has a working desk and a sitting area with overstuffed chairs and ottomans. Bathrooms feature Carrara marble, brass fixtures and towel racks, and a basket of special toiletries. Each room has four telephones (beside the bed, on the desk, in the sitting area, and in the bathroom) and a television hidden away in a cabinet. In the closet are plush terry cloth robes and an umbrella for rainy days.

The suites, including the Presidential Suite, which occupies the entire twelfth floor, are filled with antiques, English oil paintings from the eighteenth and nineteenth centuries, and Oriental carpets on the hardwood floors. The rooms have the air of a beautifully appointed country home. Each suite also has a small wet bar with complimentary setups.

Three small conference rooms on the mezzanine can accommodate twelve to forty-five people for private dinners or small meetings. All are decorated in a gray and burgundy plaid, with wood-paneled doors, brass accoutrements, and nature prints on the walls.

A full-time concierge presides over the small but elegant lobby and offers a range of services to guests, from making airline and dinner reservations to sewing on a button. Her domain is filled with English antiques (mahogany Chippendale mirrors, a Pembroke table, and Regency bookcases) and accented with fresh flowers and original oils. Here guests gather to read their complimentary morning newspapers or socialize over an English tea in the afternoon.

The Lancaster Grille, on the first floor of the hotel, is a favorite gathering spot of Houstonians. As in the rest of the hotel, the colors here are predominantly forest green accented with dark wood and brass. Two sides of the restaurant have multipaned showcase windows under burgundy awnings. Though the windows face the street, the restaurant is a cool, quiet spot even on the hottest Texas days.

The restaurant features Continental and American cuisine such as crab royal or breast of chicken Siam for lunch and red snapper Stefano en papillote, Dover sole, or grilled duck for dinner. Tables are set with gleaming white cloths, red and white china, and fresh flowers in silver vases.

The Auditorium Hotel, as it was originally known, was touted as Houston's most modern hotel when it was built in 1926. It boasted two double-speed elevators, circulating ice water (early air-conditioning), and ceiling fans in every room. Regular guests included theatrical stars performing at the neighboring Majestic and Palace theaters, as well as the top-billed wrestlers from the City Auditorium, which no longer exists.

During World War II, the basement of the hotel became the USO-operated Circus Club, a popular spot with servicemen. The grand reopening in 1983 was an all-out affair. The guest of honor was the mayor of Lancaster, England, Geoffrey Bryan, in his full robes and chains of office.

Getting There: Take Interstate 45 south to the McKinney Street exit. Go two blocks to Louisiana and turn left. Go another four blocks to Texas and turn right. The hotel is on the corner of Louisiana and Texas. If you take a bus from the airport, the hotel will pick you up from terminus in town.

GALVESTON

The Port of Galveston sits at the eastern end of a thirty-two-mile-long barrier-reef island in the Gulf of Mexico. Although Galveston's heyday as a port ended after the hurricane of 1900, ships still move up the ten-mile channel that connects the deep, natural harbor with the gulf. The island, discovered in 1528 by the Spanish, was named for Bernardo de Galvez, the eighteenth-century count in charge of Spain's territorial possessions in the Caribbean. The harbor became a haven for pirates like Jean Laffite, who used it as his headquarters between 1817 and 1821. It was a commercial center later in the century, cornering the world trade in cotton. By 1900 Galveston was one of the busiest ports in the South, rivaling even New Orleans, as well as a wealthy, cosmopolitan town. Sarah Bernhardt performed at the Opera House, as did George M. Cohan and Anna Pavlova.

The Strand, named after the London thoroughfare, was known in the 1800s as the "Wall Street of the Southwest." For several blocks along the wharf, banks, insurance companies, wholesale shippers, customs offices, and cotton factors were housed in what today is the largest collection of restored iron-front Victorian commercial buildings in the United States.

Then, in September of 1900, a hurricane hit the island with such force that it ended forever Galveston's supremacy as a port. Six thousand people were killed and half the structures were destroyed or severely damaged.

Vowing no storm would destroy them again, the islanders enlisted the help of the Army Corps of Engineers to build a 4½-mile-long seawall along the southern side of the island. Then came the Great Raising. The bay was dredged and the sludge pumped onto the island, raising the level of the city by some seven feet. Those houses not put on stilts were buried up to the second floor. Later the seawall was extended to a total length of ten miles, with a wide boulevard along the top.

Today Galveston has almost a split personality. The Seawall is crowded with modern luxury hotels, resorts, and beachfront shops selling T-shirts and shells. The leeward side of the island, mercifully spared in the storm, is more sedate. Three historic districts—The Strand, the forty-block East End District, and the smaller Silk Stocking District—represent architecture that dates from before the Civil War to the first decade of the twentieth century. The styles range from Greek, Roman, and Romanesque to Renaissance Revival, Italianate, and Victorian.

Some of the homes, such as the Aston Villa and the Bishop's Palace, are open for tours. Others have become bed-and-breakfast inns, but most are still private residences. Home tours are conducted in the spring, and there is a candlelight tour at Christmastime.

The Grand Opera House, built in 1894, has been restored and again provides a backdrop for events like the ballet. Live theater is presented throughout the year by a local theater company.

The Strand is once again Galveston's commercial district. The cotton barons have been replaced by modern merchants, and stores of every description make shopping a major event. Just a block away from the Strand towers the 103-foot mast of the *Elissa*. Tours are conducted on this 1877 iron barque, one of the tall ships that sailed into New York Harbor to celebrate Lady Liberty's hundredth birthday. Just a few yards down the wharf is *The Colonel*, an old paddlewheeler, available for narrated cruises of the harbor and for dinner cruises in the evening. Other attractions include deep-sea fishing charters and an excellent railroad museum.

The biggest event on the Galveston calendar occurs the first weekend in December, when the streets around the Strand are closed off and peddlers, dressed in costumes of the mid-nineteenth century, sell roasted chestnuts and hot plum pudding. Carolers stroll the streets, and friends toast one another with hot mugs of wassail. This extravaganza, called Dickens on the Strand, began as a small dinner party in 1973. It has since blossomed into a street party that attracts thousands, and all who join in the spirit of the festivities and come dressed in appropriate costume are admitted free of charge. Other events during the year include Mardi Gras (the week before Lent) and the Blessing of the Shrimp Fleet in April.

Getting There: Galveston is 50 miles south of Houston via Interstate 45.

The amenities of the Tremont House, just a block off the Strand, are Old World. The concierge will arrange theater tickets or a tee time for you, and have the chauffeur-driven London taxi take you there and bring you back. Besides its elegant setting and exemplary service, the Tremont has a fascinating history. Sam Houston gave his last public speech from the balcony of the first Tremont House, and both Confederate and Union soldiers were quartered there before it was destroyed by fire in 1865.

The second Tremont House, built in 1872, was the center of Galveston social activity. The guest register included the signatures of Ulysses S. Grant, Edwin Booth, Anna Pavlova, and Buffalo Bill Cody. When the hurricane of 1900 hit Galveston, the hotel served as headquarters for Clara Barton and the Red Cross, and hundreds of storm victims sought refuge at the Tremont. Though it survived the hurricane, the hotel eventually closed and was torn down in 1928.

The third and present Tremont House, located half a block from where the second hotel stood, opened its doors in February, 1985. The block-long, neo-Renaissance structure was built in 1879 as a wholesale dry-goods establishment. It was restored by native Galvestonians George and Cynthia Mitchell.

The exquisitely appointed hotel takes its color scheme from the black-and-white floor tiles in the lobby and the Adonidia palms that thrive beneath the skylight in the center of the hotel. These cool colors are accented with the warmth of hardwood floors and antiques, such as the old map cabinet that is now the bellman's desk, and the ornately carved concierge's desk.

The rooms, located on the three floors above the atrium lobby, are also done in black and white. The beds (queens in the atrium rooms, kings in the outside rooms) are custom crafted in white enamel and brass and luxuriously covered with triple sheets. The hardwood floors are covered by specially woven white-and-black rugs, and massive, custom-made armoires house remote-control televisions and pull-out desks. The black-and-white color scheme is continued in the private baths with their hand-painted Italian tiles and matching shower curtains. Plush towels are warmed on heated chrome racks, and baskets of toiletries sit on the vanities. The seven sitting-room suites are named for flowers like Magnolia; some have original brick walls and baths of Italian marble.

Glass "bird cage" elevators give guests a view of the geometric patterns of the atrium, with its white wicker furniture and glass-topped tables where afternoon tea is served. On weekends a champagne hour is held in the Toujouse Bar, so named because the ornate mirrored rosewood bar dating from 1888 came from Henry Toujouse's saloon, which had stood next to the second Tremont House.

TREMONT HOUSE

2300 Ship's Mechanic Row, Galveston, Texas 77550

Telephone: (409) 763-0300 or (800) 874-2300

Accommodations: 107 rooms with queen- or king-size beds; private baths with tub/shower; telephones; television.

Rates: expensive to very expensive, no meals included. Restaurant open for breakfast, lunch, and dinner. Children welcome. No pets.

Cards: AE, CB, DC, MC, V

Nonsmoking rooms available. Some rooms equipped for the handicapped. Open all year.

Tremont House

On weekend evenings a pianist entertains guests, and those with rooms opening onto the atrium can hear strains of semiclassical music drifting through the air and the trickle of the fountain in the Merchant Prince, a small, casual restaurant just off the lobby. Open for breakfast, lunch, and dinner, the restaurant centers around a koi-filled fountain. Lunch ranges from spinach salad to steak with bearnaise sauce; the dinner menu includes such items as cassolette of oysters and scallops, and medallions of veal.

For more formal dining, The Wentletrap, named for a shell found on Galveston beaches, is just across the alley on the Strand. Another of the Mitchells' restoration projects, and also built around an atrium, The Wentletrap is housed in a Renaissance Revival building constructed in 1871 of Houston brick with a cast-iron facade. The restaurant is open for lunch and dinner and Sunday brunch, and the service is as superb as the Continental cuisine. Both the hotel and The Wentletrap have conference facilities.

The Tremont House also has health spa, pool, and racquet club facilities available at one of the Mitchell properties on the Seawall.

Getting There: Take Broadway to Twenty-third Street (also Tremont Street) and turn left. Go to the last stoplight and turn left; the hotel is on the corner of Twenty-third and Ship's Mechanic Row. Regular limousine service from Houston's Hobby Airport to Galveston is available for a fee.

763-1141 ELENOR

On March 11, 1864, Captain Robert Stanley Guy, of the Confederate States of America, wrote a letter to his family that began: "My Dear Children, I am now away down here only about seven miles from the beautiful City of Galveston and in full view of it. This place is called Virginia Point. It is a point of land running into the Bay of Galveston." Guy survived the Civil War and later became a Texas state senator.

When Guy's great-grandson, Tom Catlow, and his wife, Eleanor, bought the old Hawley House in Galveston with plans to open a B&B, they chose to name it Virginia Point Inn, preserving a bit of family history. Guests at the inn may even read the original letter, which is kept in a glass-topped display table in the living room.

The neo-Mediterranean-style inn is located just a block off the main street of Galveston, about halfway between the beach and the historic Strand. The original cypress and birch siding has been stuccoed and painted a soft gray with burgundy touches. Shaded by live oaks and palms, the house sits amid a half-acre of meticulously maintained gardens.

THE VIRGINIA POINT INN
2327 Avenue K, + 24th.
Galveston, Texas 77550
Telephone: (409) 763-2450

Accommodations: five rooms with twin, three-quarter, double, or king-size beds; private bath in the Master Suite, others shared, with tub/shower; no telephones; no television.

Rates: expensive to very expensive, hearty Continental breakfast included. Children over twelve welcome. No pets.

Cards: AE, CB, DC, MC, V

No smoking in bedrooms or dining room. Open all year.

The house was built in 1907 for Harry Hawley, a customs broker, on three city lots adjacent to the 1868 Italianate home of a millionaire industrialist named Davis. Davis' daughter Sarah married Harry Hawley, and their home remained in the family until the Catlows purchased it. Some of the rooms are furnished with Catlow and Hawley family heirlooms (including twelve antique clocks) augmented with pieces the Catlows bought in England especially for the inn. The most unusual pieces were found in the attic: two intricately carved rosewood chairs, purchased by young Hawley and his bride on a trip to China with his in-laws. These chairs now grace the music room; Tom even has a picture of the Davis-Hawley family on rickshaws during their trip.

The floors are all edge-grain pine, and most of the floor-to-ceiling windows open to screened porches. There is a fireplace in the living room, and Tom's mother's piano is in the music room with its lace curtains and rose-colored walls.

Beyond is the dining room, its English table set with silver service and a candelabra. Eleanor serves breakfast here, or, if you prefer, on your own private balcony. Usual fare includes juice, coffee, croissants, rolls, fresh fruit, meat, and eggs. For early risers, coffee is freshly brewed by six-thirty.

In the evenings the Catlows entertain with complimentary cheese, biscuits, and wine served in glasses that came with the house. In fact, much of what is now in the butler's pantry (including the 1932 Frigidaire, which still works) was already in the house.

The guest rooms all have private screened porches and, like the rest of the house, have family heirlooms. All rooms contain marble-topped dressers, Persian or Chinese carpets, quilts, and a basket of French bath salts, sachets, and soaps.

The bed in the E. S. Guy Room belonged to Tom's grandparents and is covered with a Battenburg lace spread that matches the curtains. This room shares a large bath with the Sunrise Room, which has twin spindle beds that can be made into a king. The Blue Room has exquisite lace curtains that came with the house, a high, carved headboard, and blue quilts and comforters on the bed.

All the furniture in the R. S. Guy Room belonged to the captain, including the three-quarter spindle bed and the trunk where the letter and pictures were found. This is the smallest of the rooms. By contrast, the Master Suite is a large corner room with a fireplace and a private bath containing an old narrow tub.

The Catlows will loan guests bicycles, and croquet and badminton are available on the back lawn.

Getting There: Take Broadway into town. Turn right on Twenty-fourth to Avenue K. The inn is on the left, on the corner.

On summer evenings, owner-host Dan Dyer will pack wine and cheese in a picnic basket and arrange for a horse and carriage to pick up guests at his inn for a sunset tour of Galveston's historic districts. This romantic interlude recalls the love story that surrounds the origins of the house. The tale began in the cathedral in Cologne, Germany, where German-born Galveston businessman Samuel Maas heard Isabella Offenbach sing and fell in love with her. Maas returned to Galveston to amass a fortune as a ship chandler, and returned to Germany in 1884 to ask Isabella (the daughter of the Rabbi of Cologne and sister of the famous composer Jacques Offenbach) for her hand.

She did marry Maas and returned with him to Galveston. Their first home was destroyed in the fire of 1885, which burned a forty-block swath from the bay to the gulf. But the Maases rebuilt their home in 1887 in a Queen Anne style with Eastlake motifs. Here they raised their four children, and Isabella became known for her philanthropic work in the community. Her tireless efforts during smallpox and yellow-fever epidemics were described as heroic. Then, in 1891, after exposure to inclement weather while bringing cheer to the needy at Christmas, Isabella died.

For thirty-odd years Dr. W. C. Fisher owned the house before selling it to Cecilia Matali, wife of Amadeo Alabart Matali, a local building and cement contractor whose name is stamped in many of the sidewalks in town. He added the kitchen and the large first-floor bath, and enclosed the front second-story porch. He also constructed the cement benches and bird bath in the front yard for his wife, who was fond of birds.

Dan Dyer and Jim Wellman bought the Matali place in 1983. Dan feels that one charm of an old house is a clutter of things to look at, so trinkets, bric-a-brac, and Victoriana are scattered about. The front doors are faux-bois cypress, the stained-glass above the stairway landing is original, and the wainscoting along the stairway is of now-extinct curly pine. Among several fireplaces in the house is one in the sitting room with a beautifully carved cherry mantlepiece.

The three guest rooms on the second floor are named for the original owners. The Fisher Room (once a kitchen after Matali made the house into a duplex) is bright with flowered paper, white bedspreads, and eyelet pillows. The Offenbach Room is feminine with lace curtains, rattan chairs, and twin beds. The Maas Room, largest of the three, has a king-size bed, a mahogany fireplace (not in working order), a writing desk, and a settee tucked into a small alcove. The large shared bath has a big tub, Crabtree & Evelyn toiletries, and needlepoint decorations.

MATALI

1727 Sealy,
Galveston, Texas 77550

Telephone: (409) 763-4526

Accommodations: three rooms with twin, double, or king-size beds; shared baths with tub; no telephones; no television.

Rates: expensive, full breakfast included. Children over twelve welcome. No pets.

Cards: AE, MC V

Meeting facilities. National Register. Open all year.

Matali

The rooms are all connected and can be configured into suites. A balcony off the back of the house offers a view of the Bishop's Palace and other Victorian treasures, as well as a second-century B.C. Roman bust in the garden next door. There is a game and music room where guests may crank up the old Victrola or play a few songs on the piano.

Dan and Jim provide a wine and cheese tray in the evening. Breakfast is hearty, usually consisting of sausage, eggs, bacon, and fruit served in the formal dining room. The butler's pantry has a water cooler, refrigerator, and coffee maker for guests' use.

The horse-and-buggy ride or limousine tour is not included in the price of a room, but the inn does provide complimentary tickets for the Galveston Flyer Trolley car, which stops at the front door and takes passengers on a tour of the island, beachfront, historic Strand, and major museums. Inn guests also have membership privileges at Key Largo on the Seawall, where complete pool, Jacuzzi tub, and sauna facilities are available. The inn has bicycles for guests' use, too.

Getting There: Take Broadway to Eighteenth Street. Turn left and go one block to Sealy. The inn is on the right, on the corner, with the three flags flying on the porch.

The Victorian Inn is a beautiful example of the fine detailing executed by nineteenth-century craftsmen: The yellow maple floors in the front parlor are laid in geometric patterns to match the curve of the bay windows; the dining room is highlighted by the bird's-eye maple wainscoting and maple floors; the five carved-oak fireplaces are fronted with Belgian tiles; and the pocket doors between the downstairs rooms have ornately etched brass hardware.

Light from crystal chandeliers shimmers over the intricately carved oak stair rails. Original Victorian art glass still decorates the front windows, and a stained-glass window on the landing scatters rainbows in the upstairs hallway. The entryway has an inglenook with curved brackets, spindled fretwork, and a columned fireplace supporting an overmantel decorated with wood appliqués.

The red brick Italianate mansion that houses this artistry was built in 1899 for Isaac Heffron, a prominent cement contractor whose achievements included construction of the first Galveston seawall. Although the house was already completed when the hurricane hit Galveston in 1900, the Heffrons did not move in until early in 1901. It remained their home until 1943 when another hurricane hit, this time damaging the house.

THE VICTORIAN INN

511 Seventeenth Street, Galveston, Texas 77550

Telephone: (409) 762-3235

Accommodations: four rooms and one suite with twin or king-size beds; private and shared baths; no telephones; no television.

Rates: expensive to very expensive, Continental breakfast included. Children over twelve welcome. No pets.

Cards: AE, MC, V

Meeting facilities. National Register. Open all year.

131

The 1940s were a wild and rowdy era in Galveston. During this time, the original dual gas-and-electric chandeliers were replaced with crystal, and the decor was redone in garish colors. The house passed through the hands of several owners, then stood empty until 1977 when it was restored; it opened as a B&B four years later.

The guest rooms are on the second floor, where everything is built at an angle—some of the closets are actually triangular. Since the house was built before air-conditioning, all the rooms open to each other to make the most of the ocean breezes. Each room has access to a screened porch via walk-through windows; two porches are private, two rooms share a third.

Most of the rooms have king-size reproduction brass beds, but the armoires, marble-topped tables, and chairs are authentic Victorian pieces. Period touches include eyelet bedspreads, printed wallpapers, and the original ceiling fans. One room has a worktable, another a writing desk. Still another room has a small "trunk room," making it a small suite, perfect for a couple traveling with a third adult or a child. The Master Suite, done in sunny yellow and white, has its own private screened-in circular porch filled with white wicker furniture. The four rooms on the second floor share two large baths, one with a tub under a stained-glass window.

The third floor has been remodeled into a large suite under the dormered roof. The walls are covered in reproduction turn-of-the-century paper, but the furniture is mostly modern, though the bedroom does have a brass bed with blue chintz cover, a fainting couch, and an armoire. This is the only room with a private bath, which is quite small, and rather unusual because of the window in the shower.

The first-floor parlor is furnished in traditional Victorian pieces set in front of the carved and tiled fireplace, the only one of the five fireplaces that still works.

Guests are served a buffet-style Continental breakfast in the dining room. Usual fare includes coffee or tea, cold cereals, croissants, muffins, applesauce-oatmeal bread, and fruit in season. The curve of the dining room windows matches the arc of the circular porch where guests often take their early-morning coffee. The butler's pantry has been transformed into a coffee bar where guests may help themselves to that first cup.

The house stands on two and a half acres of land amid twenty-foot palm trees, which give it a tropical air. The perimeter of the grounds is marked with the original cement fences and wrought-iron gates. The house has a very open feeling and is popular with Galvestonians for weddings and receptions.

The inn sits just on the edge of the East End Historical District and is included in the walking tour.

Getting There: Take Broadway into town. Turn left on Seventeenth and go five blocks to Post Office. The inn is on the left on the corner of Seventeenth and Post Office.

Helen Handeman greets guests in the evenings with a tray of wine, cheese, and hors d'oeuvres as they settle amid the Victorian clutter and dozens of teddy bears that inhabit the Gilded Thistle. The inn's name is appropriate for the entire island of Galveston. The sturdy thistle digs its roots into seemingly inhospitable ground and flourishes along the Gulf Coast shoreline. Despite its thorns, it blossoms into a beautiful flower. So, too, the Texas pioneers sunk in roots on the island and hung on through hurricanes and fire to make Galveston flower in its "gilded age of prosperity and culture."

This tiny Victorian inn is a product of that gilded age. Built in 1893, it is formally known as the Bailey-Phillips House. John Bailey, secretary-treasurer and general manager of the Port of Galveston in its heyday, built the house on Galveston's "Grand Promenade" as a present for his wife, Laura. Bailey put in the pea gravel in the backyard and removed the back stairs from the second-story porch during the early part of the century; the Charles Lindbergh baby had just been kidnapped, and these measures were part of Bailey's attempt to protect his own young son. The gravel is still there and the stairs are still missing. The landscaped gardens also contain an old cistern that has withstood its share of hurricanes. In the early days, these cisterns were the only source of fresh water for island families.

The house's second owner was Ben Phillips, heir to his uncle William Parr's shipping company, the oldest in the state of Texas. The house was the scene of many a chamber-music recital by the group that young Phillips organized.

Helen Handeman, a native of Austin, bought the house in 1977 and transformed it into a haven for guests in 1982. The tiny Queen Anne boasts three oak fireplaces, curly-pine and cypress wainscoting, and screened wraparound verandas facing the gulf breezes. The bay windows in the living room are covered with lace curtains, the floors with Oriental carpets. The furniture is mostly antique; some belongs to Helen and some to her son Patrick, who helps run the inn.

The three guest rooms are on the second floor. The Master Suite, the only one with a private bath, also has a curved bay with lace curtains at the window. Helen has placed a settee, chairs, and a table here to make a sitting area. Lying on the pillows of the four-poster bed is one of the dozens of house bears, this one tiny and dressed in a long lace gown; another sits in a child's rocking chair.

The Umbrella Room is named for the grouping of Chinese paper parasols that hang from the ceiling over the plantation desk. The carved walnut bed is Eastlake, and walk-through windows open onto a sleeping porch. The Treetop Room, once the nursery, is a sunny place done in browns with an original Victorian lithograph on

GILDED THISTLE

1805 Broadway,
Galveston, Texas 77550

Telephone: (409) 763-0194

Accommodations: three rooms with double beds; private and shared baths with shower or tub/shower; telephone with long cord in the hall; television.

Rates: very expensive, hearty Continental breakfast included. Children over twelve welcome. No pets.

Cards: MC, V

Open all year.

133

Gilded Thistle

the wall; its focal point is the lacy canopy over the bed. This room and the Umbrella Room share a modern bath with a shower curtain that looks like a circus tent; clown pictures carry out the theme.

Coffee and juice are left outside your door at seven in the morning, and breakfast is offered at your convenience either on the veranda or in the dining room. Served with china, silver, and crystal, it usually consists of melon, banana bread, preserves, biscuits, eggs, sausage, and bacon. Munchies, such as Helen's brownielike "chewies," are always available on the sideboard.

Helen believes that if one lavishes guests with hospitality, they will always come back, and so far her philosophy has proved true: Guests keep returning to the Gilded Thistle.

Getting There: The inn is on Broadway just past Nineteenth Street.

Michael is Mary Michael Isbell, and she goes by Mikey. The house is the Hans Guldman Mansion, one of the many buildings in Galveston that truly deserve the title "mansion." The grounds once included a tennis court, pigeon coop, dog kennels, and an arbor of grapes that Mrs. Guldman harvested for her homemade wine. The greenhouse, where she raised ferns, begonias, and tropical plants, is an ornate Victorian folly that still stands at the back of the house. It had its own furnace and adjustable glass windows. Beside the greenhouse were the dovecote and a small fish pond.

The massive red-brick house with green ceramic-tile roof sits on just over an acre of grounds. The first three stories had already been built when the hurricane of 1915 hit the island. The mansion survived, but Guldman wanted to make sure it would survive anything a Gulf Coast hurricane could throw at it. He tore down what had already been built and constructed a fortress. Thick pillars support the building, and concrete reinforcements reach out into the grounds. Guldman even went so far as to pack all the damaged concrete from the first structure under the front yard, creating a protective slope of ground down from the house.

The mansion was built for entertaining, since Guldman was not only a successful exporter of cotton (the company he founded still exists in his native Denmark), but vice-consul for Denmark. He and his wife often hosted foreign dignitaries, and the annual Cotton Seed Crushers Convention was held at the Guldman Mansion. It is said that on occasion, Mrs. Guldman would string the entire yard with Japanese lanterns and hire an orchestra to entertain her guests. Hans died in

MICHAEL'S BED AND BREAKFAST

1715 Thirty-fifth Street, Galveston, Texas 77550

Telephone: (409) 763-3760

Accommodations: three rooms with double or king-size beds; shared baths with tub; no telephones; no television.

Rates: expensive, hearty Continental breakfast and dessert in the evening included. Children over twelve welcome. No pets.

Cards: MC, V

Smoking only in public areas. Meeting facilities. Open all year.

1932, his wife in 1977, and the house remained in the Guldman family until 1984, when Mikey and Allen Isbell bought it for a bed-and-breakfast inn.

The kitchen and the small breakfast room have been updated with Italian tiles, but Mikey has kept the rest of the house much as it must have once been. There is an open feeling about the place, with spare furnishings, few rugs on the oak floors, and no curtains in the wide downstairs windows. The dining-room table was Mikey's grandmother's, and the Texas primitive desk in the entry hall was made by Allen's great-great-grandfather. All the bronzes and paintings are original works of art. The enormous entryway has a fireplace and a mahogany staircase, favored by local brides for gracefully sweeping down in their white gowns. Perhaps the reason there are so many weddings here is that Allen is a minister and performs many of the ceremonies.

Despite the mansion's size, there are only three guest rooms on the second floor, with pine floors and a shared bath. The child's safety railing at the top of the stairs was put there for the original Guldman children, two girls and one boy, who were tutored at home by a live-in nanny. The room she used has its own pedestal sink and an iron, quilt-covered bed. The School Room is more modern in decor, with flowered curtains, matching coverlet, and a gas-log fireplace. The old school desk came from a college in Terrell, Texas, and the brass curtain rods were found in the backyard. The Pink Room is furnished with Allen's grandmother's bedroom suite, a short four-poster bed and dresser.

Breakfast is served buffet-style in the dining room and usually consists of blueberry waffles, fruit, and muffins. In the evenings, Mikey serves dessert after guests have returned from dinner in town.

The house is available for gatherings and parties and can accommodate up to fifty for an afternoon event.

Getting There: Take Broadway to Thirty-fifth. Turn right. The house is on the right between O and P streets.

LOWER
RIO GRANDE
VALLEY

RIO GRANDE CITY

SAN JUAN

PORT ISABEL

LOWER RIO GRANDE VALLEY

Like migratory birds, thousands of Texans head south for the winter, hence the epithet "Winter Texans" heard all over the Lower Rio Grande Valley. This is the southernmost tip of Texas. Here, the Rio Grande, after marking the border between the United States and Mexico for over 1,200 miles, empties into the Gulf of Mexico.

In this semitropical land, the temperature rarely dips below 50° F even in January, the coldest month of the year. Palm trees wave in the warm air, and the landscape is covered with blooming plants, including bright yellow esperanza and red poinsettia.

Often called La Frontera, the Lower Rio Grande Valley is a blend of cultures, and Spanish is heard as often as English. Indeed, the Spanish were here first, as early as 1519, when Alonzo de Pineda discovered the mouth of the Rio Grande. Other Spanish explorers followed, some on the never-ending search for gold. Centuries later, this part of Texas was included in a land grant known as El Fronton.

Over the years, this remote area has been plagued by pirates, bandits, and cattle rustlers. Battles were waged here during both the Mexican War and the American Civil War. The lighthouse at Port Isabel, built in 1852, was taken and retaken by Union troops during the Civil War, and finally abandoned in 1905. Fifty years later, the lighthouse became the smallest state park in Texas.

The Queen Isabella Causeway—Texas's longest bridge—links Port Isabel to South Padre Island, which stretches 113 miles up the Gulf Coast. Storms wrecked many a Spanish gold ship off this strip of land, and it's rumored that pirates like Jean Lafitte buried treasure on the island. Originally called Isla de Corpus Christi, the island was renamed Padre in the nineteenth century when Padre Nicholas Balli acquired it from Charles IV of Spain for about four hundred pesos.

Today, the treasure of Padre Island lies in the undeveloped eighty-mile stretch of National Seashore in the central part of the island and in the sandy beaches filled with vacationers. Besides the natural beauty of the area, there are other attractions, such as the renowned Gladys Porter Zoo in Brownsville. For aviation buffs, the Confederate Air Force, a display of World War II combat aircraft at the Harlingen Airport, is on view all year, but the big event is the air show in October. For the more adventurous, fascinating shopping awaits just across the border in Matamoros.

Getting There: Several airlines fly into both McAllen and Harlingen. Rental cars are available at both airports.

The area around Rio Grande City was originally part of a Spanish land grant given to Captain José Antonio de la Garza Falcón by the King of Spain in 1767. In 1848, after Zachary Taylor established nearby Fort Ringgold, Rio Grande City became an important post on the Mexican border.

In 1893 the successful merchant François LaBorde, homesick for New Orleans, had Paris architects design a home with iron filigree reminiscent of the French Quarter. The brick building, trimmed with green wrought-iron gingerbread, was completed in 1899 and often served as a way station for travelers: military officers on their way to California, cattle barons who sold their herds on the nearby river docks, and travelers who came by riverboat and wagon.

Eventually, LaBorde added a second story to the building and another two-story structure at the front; the space between became a patio. Then in 1917, at age fifty and for no apparent reason, François LaBorde killed himself.

The house remained in the family until 1939, when it was purchased by George R. Boyle, the geologist who discovered the Fordice Vanderbilt Fault during the oil boom in the Lower Rio Grande Valley. He changed the name to The Ringgold, added seventeen baths, and rented the rooms for four dollars a day. Most of his lodgers were Laredo salesmen, until the oil ran out.

In 1980 the hotel was rescued by Larry Sheerin of San Antonio. Using original records and photographs, and consulting with the Texas Historical Society, he made the restoration as authentic as possible—no mean feat.

The inside, except for the floors, was gutted. All the woodwork on the walls, stairs, and windows was replaced. The double-hung windows were rebuilt with their original nine-over-six pane configurations, and the stair banisters were recarved by hand, as the originals had been. The adobe was repainted, and replacement bricks were made in the same brickyard in Camargo, Mexico, as the originals. All missing and damaged gingerbread trim was recut and matched on site by local craftsmen; much of the wrought-iron fence was reforged; and the wooden galleries on three sides of the building were rebuilt.

Today, guests enter the hotel through a plant-filled courtyard with a stone fountain. The gates are flanked by horse-head hitching posts and lit at night by globe streetlights. The front of the hotel houses the eight "grand bedrooms," furnished with turn-of-the-century antiques that Larry Sheerin collected all over the West and the South. Many of the wallpapers and fabrics are the same as those used in the restoration of the Texas Governor's Mansion. The floors are covered in Axminster or Oriental carpets, and the private baths have floors and walls of Mexican tiles.

LABORDE HOUSE

601 Main Street,
Rio Grande City, Texas 78582

Telephone: (512) 487-5101

Accommodations: eight "grand bedrooms" and thirteen modern rooms with twin or double beds; private baths with tub, shower, or tub/shower; no telephones; television.

Rates: inexpensive to moderate, Continental breakfast included. Restaurant open for lunch and dinner, closed Sunday. Children welcome. Small, well-behaved pets allowed.

Cards: AE, MC, V

Wheelchair access by elevator. Meeting facilities. National Register. Open all year.

LaBorde House

Each room's name commemorates a bit of local history: LaBorde is a large room with a carved headboard on the bed, an oval mirror over the dresser, and Oriental carpets. Over the fireplace, which is now just for show, is an elaborately carved mantle. The bath has a claw-foot tub and a wide pedestal sink. Audubon, done in yellows, has twin beds and a claw-foot tub set behind a screen in the room. Rio Grande also has twin beds, in brass, and a tiny bath with tiled shower. Maria Tejas has a four-poster covered with pleated satin.

Recamara Roja, entered from the front balcony, is dominated by an ornate half-tester draped in red silk. It also boasts a red-and-white Axminster carpet and a love seat upholstered in red. This room has a tiny kitchenette behind shuttered doors, and a large bath.

The Law Office was once just that. Its unusual features include a glass case behind the bed filled with old leather-bound law books, a "chest of drawers" that opens into a second bed, a rolltop desk, Oriental carpets, and a pressed-tin ceiling.

Downstairs, off the long hallway leading back to the patio, is a spacious, elegant parlor filled with antiques gathered into small conversation groups. Here time passes quietly, the hours tolled by the rich tones of the grandfather clock in the hall. The floor-to-ceiling, glass-fronted bookcase is filled with local reference material, which guests are welcome to read.

The only sound in the brick-paved courtyard is the trickle of water from the tiled, lion-head fountain. The hotel often caters special functions for groups of fifty to seventy-five in this patio, which is filled with plants and tiled tables. At the back of the courtyard are thirteen efficiency apartments with Murphy beds and small kitchenettes.

Also off this patio is Che's Restaurant, which serves lunch and dinner in the courtyard or in the oak-paneled dining room, which is accented with forest-green rugs, beveled glass, rattan furniture, and a profusion of plants. The food is "border cuisine": steak, fried Rio Grande catfish, and fajitas; the vegetables are grown on nearby farms.

Located eighty miles northwest of Harlingen, the LaBorde House is just a block from the Mexican border. Rio Grande City is most famous for its replica of the Grotto of Lourdes in the churchyard, but nearby there is also golf, hunting, water sports at Falcon Lake Recreation Area, and shopping in Camargo, Mexico. Monterrey is an easy day trip.

Getting There: From Harlingen or McAllen, take Highway 83 west to Rio Grande City. Turn left at the first road after the fourth stoplight. The hotel is on the corner of the next block (Main), on the left.

John Closner, who along with a few other local men would eventually found the city of San Juan, came to Texas with Jay Gould's railroad expansion. Gould's railroad failed, but change still came to south Texas. The San Juan Plantation experimented with irrigated farming, and citrus trees began to flourish. The Spanish Colonial–style San Juan Hotel was built in 1919, about the time Midwesterners began coming south in "land parties." These prospective residents of the Rio Grande Valley arrived by train, stayed at the San Juan Hotel across the street from the depot, and took convoys out to the citrus groves in search of property. Eventually many of them settled in the valley.

In its heyday the hotel was a social gathering place; there was even a band shell where weekly dances were held. Eventually the hotel fell into disuse, and after it was finally abandoned in 1958, vandals took everything they could carry.

When the Sigles bought the old derelict in 1981, there were no windows and no doors, and the ceiling was lying on what was once the floor. Today the exterior looks much the same as it did in the old days, but it took twenty months to redo the interior, including the addition of bathrooms to each room. Glenn Sigle, a builder by trade, is retired from the hotel business, which he conducted with his wife, Mary. Their son David is a restoration architect who worked in the French Quarter of New Orleans and now runs the hotel.

The community was supportive throughout the restoration. Many townspeople came with gifts of doorknobs and other small items from the old hotel. A hand-carved desk, which had been a gift to the owners in 1940, was returned and now sits in the lobby. The worn brick that paves the lobby floor was made at the San Juan Plantation about 1915 and was salvaged from the town's first brick building, which was demolished about the time the hotel was being restored. The tiled, raised fireplace houses the TV in warm months, and rattan and wooden furniture is clustered into conversation groups. A glass case displays some of the artifacts found on the site, including Wallace silver once used in the dining room.

Behind the lobby is a brick-paved courtyard with a wishing well and bougainvilleas, palms, Turk's-cap lilies, plumbagos, and banana and papaya trees. A black-painted swimming pool has its own separate courtyard at the side of the hotel.

Facing the main courtyard are twenty-two rooms, each furnished with three or four antique pieces augmented with reproductions. All rooms have wall-to-wall carpeting, televisions, telephones, ceiling fans, air-conditioning, and heating. Mexican tile decorates the bathrooms.

The decor is reminiscent of the 1920s. The shutters over the windows, to keep out the fierce summer sun, were handmade by Glenn. Some of the wooden beds are

SAN JUAN HOTEL

125 West Business 83, Box 114, San Juan, Texas 78589

Telephone: (512) 781-5339

Accommodations: twenty-two rooms with twin, double, or king-size beds; private baths with tub/shower; telephones; television.

Rates: inexpensive, no meals included. Restaurant open for breakfast, lunch, and dinner; closed Sunday night. Children welcome. Small pets allowed with advance notice.

Cards: AE, CB, DC, MC, V

Wheelchair access. Meeting facilities. Texas Medallion. Open all year.

also handmade; other beds are brass or wicker. Audubon prints and antique maps adorn the walls, and each room has an armoire or a rack for clothes.

The dining room, also off the courtyard, contains Mexican artifacts from Oaxaca that are part of a collection David began several years ago. Open for breakfast, lunch, and dinner (except Sunday dinner), the restaurant features steak, seafood, and Mexican dishes. (During the summer months the restaurant is also closed on Monday evenings.) David, a member of the Texas Chef's Association, does all the food planning. Next to the restaurant is a small, cozy coffee shop with slate floors and Indian artifacts on the walls; behind the restaurant is yet another courtyard where meals are also served.

San Juan is located three miles east of McAllen; area attractions include the Shrine to the Virgin de San Juan Del Valle, and South Padre Island, an hour away. A bird sanctuary at nearby Santa Ana National Wildlife Refuge shelters some of the last native brush in the state. From November through March, the Audubon Society offers tours of the area; the rest of the year, tours are self-guided.

Getting There: From Harlingen or McAllen, take Highway 83 west to San Juan. Take the FM 1426 exit and turn left on Nebraska (under the freeway). Go past the stoplight and turn right onto Business 83. The hotel is on your left, about half a block down. Airport service can be arranged with advance notice.

In the late 1920s, the Yacht Club Hotel was just that, a private yacht club with a membership that included most of the prominent families in the Rio Grande Valley. It was *the* place for social and weekend gatherings for South Texas society, members often dancing into the wee hours to the sound of the big bands. After the Crash of 1929, one of the owners, John Shary, bought out the others and opened the hotel to the public. For many years it retained its reputation as the fashionable place to dine, and catered to such celebrities as Charles Lindbergh.

The elegant two-story white stucco hotel with its red tiled roof withstood several major hurricanes with the loss of only one bell tower, but it did not fare so well with time. Its glory faded, and the building became a flophouse for the local shrimp fishermen. Eventually, in 1969, the hotel closed its doors. Ten years later it was rescued and renovated by Ron and Lynn Speier.

Set amid beautifully landscaped grounds, the Yacht Club Hotel is an elegant place. All twenty-four rooms face the yacht harbor across the street. The rattan furniture is new, as are the drapes and carpets. The dark paneling that still remains in

THE YACHT CLUB HOTEL
700 Yturria Street,
Port Isabel, Texas 78578

Telephone: (512) 943-1301

Accommodations: twenty-four rooms with double, queen-, or king-size beds; private baths with tub/shower; no telephones; color television.

Rates: inexpensive, Continental breakfast included. Restaurant open for dinner only, closed Wednesday. Children welcome. No pets.

Cards: AE, CB, DC, MC, V

Wheelchair access. Convention facilities. Open all year.

some of the rooms is being replaced by light painted walls. At either end of the two wings of the hotel, porches have been glassed in to make four suites, two on each floor; the living areas have glass on three sides, and the bedrooms are spacious.

The large hexagonal bell tower in the center of the hotel was once a guest room, and there are plans to make it into a honeymoon suite. All the rooms have televisions, though with the beaches and night life of South Padre Island only five minutes away, there is little incentive to stay "home."

The Yacht Club's restaurant again has a reputation as one of the finest in the area, with the most extensive wine list in South Texas. The 135 wines offered are mostly from California and in the ten-dollar range, though you can buy a Mouton Rothschild or a Dom Perignon for considerably more.

The restaurant's expansion attests to its popularity; it has taken over the former lobby. In 1981 additional dining space was added to the back of the hotel, along with a pool and an enclosed courtyard filled with oleanders, hibiscus, bougainvillea, palms, ficus, and banana plants that provide the fruit for the banana daiquiris served in the bar. Sampling the seafood is a must in the Shrimp Capital of the World. Along with the shrimp, the restaurant is noted for its stuffed crab and red snapper dishes.

In keeping with the Spanish style of the hotel, the dining-room ceilings are high and dark beamed, the walls white, the carpet and drapes red, and the furniture handmade in Mexico. Clerestory windows look up at the cupola, and tables are set with pewter and china. The wall displays remind diners that they are never far from the ocean in Port Isabel: Stuffed game fish are hung alongside photographs of victorious fishermen and women. There are framed articles about the hotel and the town from old newspapers, and everywhere the wine racks display the various offerings of the extensive cellar.

In the morning, a Continental breakfast is set out in the tiny lobby for guests to take back to their rooms or to enjoy on the cool, covered patio along the front of the hotel.

Fishing charters and tours in Mexico, only twenty-five miles away, are available, and there is golf in Brownsville. Harlingen has the Confederate Air Force, South Padre Island has long stretches of beach, and it's only a short walk through town to the famous lighthouse.

This part of Texas is primarily a summer resort, so from March through September and on holidays reservations should be made well in advance.

Getting There: From Harlingen, take Highway 77 south to Highway 100 east into Port Isabel. Once in town, turn left on Yturria. The hotel is just past the curve in the road, on the right. Limousine service available from the airport for a fee.

INNS LOCATED WITHIN A NATIONAL HISTORIC DISTRICT

Country Cottage Inn, Fredericksburg, 91

Gilded Thistle, Galveston, 133

La Colombe d'Or, Houston, 120

Matali, Galveston, 129

McKay House, Jefferson, 57

Norton Brackenridge House Bed and Breakfast Inn, San Antonio, 73

Rische House, San Antonio, 72

The Excelsior House, Jefferson, 50

The Hotel Jefferson Historic Inn, Jefferson, 51

The Victorian Inn, Galveston, 131

The Virginia Point Inn, Galveston, 127

Tremont House, Galveston, 125

Wise Manor, Jefferson, 59

INN LISTED ON THE TEXAS HISTORICAL REGISTER (TEXAS MEDALLION)

Ash-Bowers Residence, Palestine, 44

Browning Plantation, Chappell Hill, 64

Country Cottage Inn, Fredericksburg, 91

Hotel Faust, New Braunfels, 110

Landmark Inn, Castroville, 111

McKay House, Jefferson, 57

Pfeiffer House, Bastrop, 103

Pride House, Jefferson, 52

Prince Solms Inn, New Braunfels, 108

Reiffert-Mugge Inn, Cuero, 114

San Juan Hotel, San Juan, 143

Stockyards Hotel, Fort Worth, 26

Tarlton House Bed and Breakfast, Hillsboro, 36

The Badu House, Llano, 94

The Bullis House Inn, San Antonio, 74

The Excelsior House, Jefferson, 50

The Gage Hotel, Marathon, 14

The Lancaster, Houston, 121

Wise Manor, Jefferson, 59

INNS LISTED ON THE NATIONAL REGISTER OF HISTORIC PLACES

Browning Plantation, Chappell Hill, 64

Hotel Faust, New Braunfels, 110

LaBorde House, Rio Grande City, 140

Landmark Inn, Castroville, 111

Matali, Galveston, 129

Pfeiffer House, Bastrop, 103

Prince Solms Inn, New Braunfels, 108

Tarlton House Bed and Breakfast, Hillsboro, 36

The Badu House, Llano, 94

The Excelsior House, Jefferson, 50

The Nutt House, Granbury, 29

The Victorian Inn, Galveston, 131

CHILDREN WELCOME

Annie's Bed and Breakfast Country Inn and Guest House, Big Sandy, 42

Aquarena Springs Inn, San Marcos, 105

Ash-Bowers Residence, Palestine, 44

Baron's Creek Inn (over 10 only), Fredericksburg, 89

Country Cottage Inn, Fredericksburg, 91

Dixie Dude Ranch, Bandera, 80

Guadalupe River Ranch, Boerne, 86

Hale House Bed and Breakfast, Jefferson, 55

Harlyn House Bed and Breakfast, Marble Falls, 96

High Cotton Inn, Bellville, 63

Hotel Faust, New Braunfels, 110

Indian Lodge, Fort Davis, 17

La Colombe d'Or, Houston, 120

LaBorde House, Rio Grande City, 140

Landmark Inn, Castroville, 111

Lazy Hills Guest Ranch, Ingram, 87

Mayan Dude Ranch, Bandera, 84

McKay House, Jefferson, 57

Norton Brackenridge House Bed and Breakfast Inn, San Antonio, 73

Pfeiffer House, Bastrop, 103

Pride House (over 10 only), Jefferson, 52

Prude Guest Ranch, Fort Davis, 21

Rische House, San Antonio, 72

San Juan Hotel, San Juan, 143

Silver Spur Guest Ranch, Bandera, 82

Stillwater Inn, Jefferson, 58

Stockyards Hotel, Fort Worth, 26

Sutler's Limpia Hotel, Fort Davis, 18

Terrell Castle, San Antonio, 77

The Bullis House Inn, San Antonio, 74

The Excelsior House, Jefferson, 50

The Gage Hotel, Marathon, 14

The Hotel Jefferson Historic Inn, Jefferson, 51

The Inn at Salado (over 10 only), Salado, 97

The Lancaster, Houston, 121

The Nutt House, Granbury, 29

The Oxford House (over 10 only), Stephenville, 31

The Thomas J. Rusk Hotel, Rusk, 47

The Yacht Club Hotel, Port Isabel, 144

Tremont House, Galveston, 125

Weimar Country Inn (over 5 only), Weimar, 67

Wise Manor, Jefferson, 59

PETS ALLOWED

High Cotton Inn (boarding can be arranged), Bellville, 63

LaBorde House (small only), Rio Grande City, 140

La Colombe d'Or, Houston, 120

Norton Brackenridge House Bed and Breakfast Inn (small only), San Antonio, 73

Prude Guest Ranch, Fort Davis, 21

San Juan Hotel (small, with advance notice), San Juan, 143

Stillwater Inn (boarding can be arranged), Jefferson, 58

Sutler's Limpia Hotel (in one room only), Fort Davis, 18

Terrell Castle (in dog run), San Antonio, 77

The Gage Hotel, Marathon, 14

The Lancaster (small only), Houston, 121

LIMITED WHEELCHAIR ACCESS

Annie's Bed and Breakfast Country Inn and Guest Ranch, Big Sandy, 42

Country Cottage Inn, Fredericksburg, 91

Guadalupe River Ranch, Boerne, 86

Hotel Faust, New Braunfels, 110

Indian Lodge, Fort Davis, 17

La Colombe d'Or, Houston, 120

Landmark Inn, Castroville, 111

Lazy Hills Guest Ranch, Ingram, 87

Mayan Dude Ranch, Bandera, 84

Prude Guest Ranch, Fort Davis, 21

San Juan Hotel, San Juan, 143

Stockyards Hotel, Fort Worth, 26

Sutler's Limpia Hotel, Fort Davis, 18

The Excelsior House, Jefferson, 50

The Hotel Jefferson Historic Inn, Jefferson, 51

The Lancaster, Houston, 121

The Yacht Club Hotel, Port Isabel, 144

Tremont House, Galveston, 125

Weimar Country Inn, Weimar, 67

SMOKING RESTRICTIONS

Annie's Bed and Breakfast Country Inn and Guest House, Big Sandy, 42

Baron's Creek Inn, Fredericksburg, 89

Browning Plantation, Chappell Hill, 64

Country Cottage Inn, Fredericksburg, 91

Hale House Bed and Breakfast, Jefferson, 55

High Cotton Inn, Bellville, 63

Inn on the River, Glen Rose, 34

Landmark Inn, Castroville, 111

Lazy Hills Guest Ranch, Ingram, 87

Lone Star Inn of Texas Bed and Breakfast, Georgetown, 98

McKay House, Jefferson, 57

Michael's Bed and Breakfast, Galveston, 135

Pfeiffer House, Bastrop, 103

Reiffert-Mugge Inn, Cuero, 114

Silver Spur Guest Ranch, Bandera, 82

Southard-House, Austin, 101

Stillwater Inn, Jefferson, 58

Tarlton House Bed and Breakfast, Hillsboro, 36

The Castle Inn, Navasota, 60

The Inn at Salado, Salado, 97

The Lancaster, Houston, 121

The Oxford House, Stephenville, 31

The Virginia Point Inn, Galveston, 127

Tremont House, Galveston, 125

FIREPLACES IN SOME OR ALL ROOMS

Country Cottage Inn, Fredericksburg, 91

Dixie Dude Ranch, Bandera, 80

Lazy Hills Guest Ranch, Ingram, 87

Mayan Dude Ranch, Bandera, 84

McKay House, Jefferson, 57

Pride House, Jefferson, 52

Southard-House, Austin, 101

Stockyards Hotel, Fort Worth, 26

Terrell Castle, San Antonio, 77

The Bullis House Inn, San Antonio, 74

The Virginia Point Inn, Galveston, 127

KITCHEN FACILITIES AVAILABLE

Aquarena Springs Inn, San Marcos, 105

Baron's Creek Inn, Fredericksburg, 89

Country Cottage Inn, Fredericksburg, 91

LaBorde House, Rio Grande City, 140

Norton Brackenridge House Bed and Breakfast Inn, San Antonio, 73

Stillwater Inn, Jefferson, 58

The Nutt House, Granbury, 29

SWIMMING POOLS ON THE PREMISES

Aquarena Springs Inn, San Marcos, 105

Browning Plantation, Chappell Hill, 64

Dixie Dude Ranch, Bandera, 80

Guadalupe River Ranch, Boerne, 86

High Cotton Inn, Bellville, 63

Indian Lodge, Fort Davis, 17

Inn on the River, Glen Rose, 34

Mayan Dude Ranch, Bandera, 84

Prude Guest Ranch, Fort Davis, 21

San Juan Hotel, San Juan, 143

Silver Spur Guest Ranch, Bandera, 82

The Yacht Club Hotel, Port Isabel, 144

SWIMMING PRIVILEGES AT ANOTHER LOCATION

Matali, Galveston, 129

The Lancaster, Houston, 121

Tremont House, Galveston, 125

GOLF NEARBY

Annie's Bed and Breakfast Country Inn and Guest House, Big Sandy, 42

Aquarena Springs Inn, San Marcos, 105

Ash-Bowers Residence, Palestine, 44

Baron's Creek Inn, Fredericksburg, 89

Country Cottage Inn, Fredericksburg, 91

Gilded Thistle, Galveston, 133

Guadalupe River Ranch, Boerne, 86

Hale House Bed and Breakfast, Jefferson, 55

Harlyn House Bed and Breakfast, Marble Falls, 96

High Cotton Inn, Bellville, 63

Hotel Faust, New Braunfels, 110

La Colombe d'Or, Houston, 120

LaBorde House, Rio Grande City, 140

Lazy Hills Guest Ranch, Ingram, 87

Lone Star Inn of Texas Bed and Breakfast, Georgetown, 98

Matali, Galveston, 129

Mayan Dude Ranch, Bandera, 84

McKay House, Jefferson, 57

Norton Brackenridge House Bed and Breakfast Inn, San Antonio, 73

Pfeiffer House, Bastrop, 103

Pride House, Jefferson, 52

Prince Solms Inn, New Braunfels, 108

Reiffert-Mugge Inn, Cuero, 114

Rische House, San Antonio, 72

San Juan Hotel, San Juan, 143

Silver Spur Guest Ranch, Bandera, 82

Southard-House, Austin, 101

Stillwater Inn, Jefferson, 58

Tarlton House Bed and Breakfast, Hillsboro, 36

Terrell Castle, San Antonio, 77

The Badu House, Llano, 94

The Bullis House Inn, San Antonio, 74

The Castle Inn, Navasota, 60

The Excelsior House, Jefferson, 50

The Gage Hotel, Marathon, 14

The Hotel Jefferson Historic Inn, Jefferson, 51

The Lancaster, Houston, 121

The Nutt House, Granbury, 29

The Thomas J. Rusk Hotel, Rusk, 47

The Victorian Inn, Galveston, 131

The Virginia Point Inn, Galveston, 127

Tremont House, Galveston, 125

Weimar Country Inn, Weimar, 67

Wise Manor, Jefferson, 59

AIRPORT TRANSPORTATION FROM MUNICIPAL AIRPORT (PRIVATE PLANES) AVAILABLE

Baron's Creek Inn, Fredericksburg, 89

Country Cottage Inn, Fredericksburg, 91

Gilded Thistle, Galveston, 133

Harlyn House Bed and Breakfast, Marble Falls, 96

LaBorde House, Rio Grande City, 140

Lazy Hills Guest Ranch, Ingram, 87

Lone Star Inn of Texas Bed and Breakfast, Georgetown, 98

Mayan Dude Ranch, Bandera, 84

Michael's Bed and Breakfast, Galveston, 135

Prince Solms Inn, New Braunfels, 108

Prude Guest Ranch, Fort Davis, 21

Reiffert-Mugge Inn, Cuero, 114

San Juan Hotel, San Juan, 143

Silver Spur Guest Ranch, Bandera, 82

Southard-House, Austin, 101

The Badu House, Llano, 94

The Lancaster, Houston, 121

The Oxford House, Stephenville, 31

The Thomas J. Rusk Hotel, Rusk, 47

The Virginia Point Inn, Galveston, 127

Weimar Country Inn, Weimar, 67

AIRPORT TRANSPORTATION AVAILABLE FOR A FEE

Guadalupe River Ranch, Boerne, 86

La Colombe d'Or, Houston, 120

Mayan Dude Ranch, Bandera, 84

Norton Brackenridge House Bed and Breakfast Inn, San Antonio, 73

Rische House, San Antonio, 72

The Virginia Point Inn, Galveston, 127

The Yacht Club Hotel, Port Isabel, 144

Tremont House, Galveston, 125

GUEST RANCHES

Dixie Dude Ranch, Bandera, 80

Guadalupe River Ranch, Boerne, 86

Lazy Hills Guest Ranch, Ingram, 87

Mayan Dude Ranch, Bandera, 84

Prude Guest Ranch, Fort Davis, 21

Silver Spur Guest Ranch, Bandera, 82

NOTES

NOTES

NOTES

YOU ARE

Never Alone

Trust in the Miracle of
GOD'S PRESENCE *and* **POWER**

MAX LUCADO

THOMAS NELSON
Since 1798

Published in Nashville, Tennessee, by Thomas Nelson. Thomas Nelson is a registered trademark of HarperCollins Christian Publishing, Inc.

Thomas Nelson titles may be purchased in bulk for educational, business, fund-raising, or sales promotional use. For information, please e-mail SpecialMarkets@ThomasNelson.com.

Any Internet addresses, phone numbers, or company or product information printed in this book are offered as a resource and are not intended in any way to be or to imply an endorsement by Thomas Nelson, nor does Thomas Nelson vouch for the existence, content, or services of these sites, phone numbers, companies, or products beyond the life of this book.

Unless otherwise noted, Scripture quotations are taken from the New King James Version®. © 1982 by Thomas Nelson. Used by permission. All rights reserved.

Scripture quotations marked AMP are from the Amplified® Bible, copyright © 1954, 1958, 1962, 1964, 1965, 1987 by The Lockman Foundation. Used by permission. (www.Lockman.org). Scripture quotations marked ESV are from the ESV® Bible (The Holy Bible, English Standard Version®), copyright © 2001 by Crossway, a publishing ministry of Good News Publishers. Used by permission. All rights reserved. Scripture quotations marked GOD'S WORD are from GOD'S WORD®, © 1995 God's Word to the Nations. Used by permission of God's Word Mission Society. Scripture quotations marked HCSB are from the Holman Christian Standard Bible®, copyright © 1999, 2000, 2002, 2003, 2009 by Holman Bible Publishers. Used by permission. HCSB® is a federally registered trademark of Holman Bible Publishers. Scripture quotations marked THE MESSAGE are from The Message. Copyright © by Eugene H. Peterson 1993, 1994, 1995, 1996, 2000, 2001, 2002. Used by permission of Tyndale House Publishers, Inc. Scripture quotations marked NCV are from the New Century Version®. © 2005 by Thomas Nelson. Used by permission. All rights reserved. Scripture quotations marked NIV are from the Holy Bible, New International Version®, NIV®. Copyright © 1973, 1978, 1984, 2011 by Biblica, Inc.™ Used by permission of Zondervan. All rights reserved worldwide. www.zondervan.com. The "NIV" and "New International Version" are trademarks registered in the United States Patent and Trademark Office by Biblica, Inc.™ Scripture quotations marked NLT are from the Holy Bible, New Living Translation. © 1996, 2004, 2007, 2013, 2015 by Tyndale House Foundation. Used by permission of Tyndale House Publishers, Inc., Carol Stream, Illinois 60188. All rights reserved. Scripture quotations marked NRSV are from the New Revised Standard Version Bible. Copyright © 1989 National Council of the Churches of Christ in the United States of America. Used by permission. All rights reserved. Scripture quotations marked PHILLIPS are from J. B. Phillips: THE NEW TESTAMENT IN MODERN ENGLISH, Revised Edition. © J. B. Phillips 1958, 1960, 1972. Used by permission of Macmillan Publishing Co., Inc. Scripture quotations marked RSV are from the Revised Standard Version of the Bible, copyright 1946, 1952, and 1971 National Council of the Churches of Christ in the United States of America. Used by permission. All rights reserved. Scripture quotations marked TLB are from The Living Bible. Copyright © 1971. Used by permission of Tyndale House Publishers, Inc., Carol Stream, Illinois 60188. All rights reserved.

ISBN: 978-1-4002-1734-2 (HC)
ISBN: 978-1-4002-2099-1 (IE)
ISBN: 978-1-4001-1735-9 (eBook)
ISBN: 978-1-4041-1478-4 (Custom)

Library of Congress Control Number: 2020938685

Printed in the United States of America
20 21 22 23 24 LSC 6 5 4 3 2 1

*Much appreciation to the following ministers,
whose faith and courage inspire our church:
Travis and Alisha Eades, Brian and Janet Carruth,
Miguel and Haydee Feria, Mario and Christina Gallegos,
Sam and Ann Gonzalez, Jimmy and Annette Pruitt,
Rich and Linda Ronald*

Contents

Acknowledgments

*H*ere is what I think happened. Long ago God decided that Lucado needed all the help heaven could muster. He knew that I would get off track, procrastinate, come down with the grumps, and waddle in the dumps and that I would require a top-notch, A1 support team that the angels themselves would envy. How else does any one person end up surrounded by such amazing folks? I don't deserve them. But I certainly love them.

Ladies and gentlemen, let me introduce you to (drumroll please) the best support team any author has ever had.

Liz Heaney and Karen Hill—No better editors exist. For the millionth time thank you.

Carol Bartley—You are to copyediting what Julia Child was to the kitchen: the greatest.

Steve and Cheryl Green—Heaven loaned you to earth, and we ain't giving you back.

The HCCP team of superheroes—Mark Schoenwald, Don Jacobson, Tim Paulson, Mark Glesne, Erica Smith, Janene MacIvor, and Laura Minchew.

Brian Hampton—a special tribute to this precious man who passed from this life to the next as this book was being completed.

David Moberg—a part of Christian publishing since 1975 and an essential part of my world since 1989. Thank you for, well, for being David Moberg.

Jana Muntsinger and Pamela McClure—Though your title is publicist, *friend* is the better word. Thank you.

Greg and Susan Ligon—You calm; you clarify; you create. Is there anything you can't do? Many thanks for keeping this train on track.

Dave Treat—Once again you lifted up this project in prayer. May your highest prayers be answered.

Janie Padilla and Margaret Mechinus—Thanks to you, calls get made, e-mails get answered, books get shelved, and chaos becomes calm.

Brett, Jenna, Rosie, Max, Andrea, Jeff, and Sara. This family tree is ever greener, vibrant, and increasingly nutty. I love each one of you.

And Denalyn, my bride. When God made you, he used the stuff of violins and fine wine. You, like them, grow sweeter with time. I love you.

CHAPTER 1

We Can't, but God Can

*I*t's just me, and I ain't much."

We'd been talking for well into an hour before she said the words. We'd worked our way through two cups of machine-brewed, hospital-waiting-room coffee. Hers with sweetener, mine with powdered creamer. Small of stature she was. No makeup, hair matted. Her T-shirt was loose fitting and crumpled. I wondered if she'd slept in it. She stirred incessantly, wheeling the plastic stick round and round until her drink became a small whirlpool akin to the emotions she was feeling—ever-spinning, circling, cycling feelings of helplessness.

Her seventeen-year-old son, who at that moment was in the intensive care unit two doors and fifty yards away, had battled opioid addiction for a year, maybe more. A car wreck had landed him in the hospital. Four days of forced detox had left him craving pills that the doctors would not provide. He was secured to the bed with restraints.

It took the mom nearly an hour to tell me what I just told you in one paragraph. Her story required sob breaks and deep sighs and included flashes of anger when referring to her ex-husband, whose presence and child support had been missing for the better part of a year. No sign of the father all week. He always had his excuses. All in all the mom believed, "It's just me, and I ain't much."

She squeezed her foam cup so tightly I thought it would crack.

Do you know this feeling? Are you acquainted with the downward spiral? Convinced that no one cares, that no one can help you, hear you, or heed your call?

If you know the feeling, you aren't alone. I don't mean you aren't alone in knowing the feeling. I mean you aren't alone. Period. That raw, dark sense of isolation and powerlessness? It's not here to stay. If you think it's up to you and you ain't much, I have some events for you to consider.

Better said, John the apostle has some stories for you to ponder. He interwove a tapestry of miracles that were "written that you may believe that Jesus is the Christ, the Son of God, and that believing you may have life in His name" (John 20:31).

Life-giving belief! This is what John wants to discuss. Abundant, robust, and resilient faith. Life happens when we believe. We find strength beyond our strength. We accomplish tasks beyond our capacity. We see solutions beyond our wisdom.

Belief is not some respectful salute to a divine being. Belief happens when we place our confidence in God. It is a decision to lean entirely upon the strength of a living and loving Savior.

To the extent we do, we will have "life in His name." This is the purpose of the miracles. John recounted signs, each one intended to stir conviction in this promise: you and I are never,

ever alone. Was this not one of the final promises of Christ? Before he ascended to heaven, he assured his friends, "I am with you always, to the end of the age" (Matt. 28:20 ESV).

Those words must have meant everything to John.

Picture the aged apostle as he shares these stories. He's an old man. Hair silver, skin wrinkled. But his eyes are full of hope, and he has a laugh that can fill a room. He pastors a collection of Christ followers in Ephesus. He loves to tell—and they love to hear—about the day some six decades earlier and a thousand miles removed when Jesus invited him to lay down the fishing net and follow him. John did.

So did Peter, Andrew, and James. They are gone now. They've long since fulfilled their missions and finished their lives. Only John remains.

And John, likely knowing his days are coming to an end, takes on one final task. Mark's gospel is in circulation. Matthew and Luke have compiled their accounts of the life of Christ. John wants to do the same. Yet his gospel will be different. He seeks to tell stories they didn't and to add details to stories they told. He selects for his gospel a cross section of "signs."

He takes us to Cana to sample some wine, then to Capernaum to watch a father embrace the son he feared would die. We feel the fury of an angry storm in Galilee and hear the murmur of a hungry crowd on a hillside. We watch a paralytic stand up and a blind man look up. Before John is done, he'll lead us through two cemeteries and near one cross and invite us to eavesdrop on a breakfast chat that changed the life of an apostle. John's chosen miracles run the gamut from a wedding oversight to a violent execution, from empty bellies to empty dreams, from abandoned hopes to buried friends. And we will be careful, oh so careful, to see the signs as John designed them to be seen, not as entries in a history book, but as samples from God's playbook.

All these events stand together as one voice, calling on you to lift your eyes and open your heart to the possibility—indeed, the reality—that the greatest force in the universe is One who means you well and brings you hope.

John recorded them, not to impress us, but to urge us to believe in the tender presence and mighty power of Christ. This montage of miracles proclaims: God's got this! Think it's up to you and you ain't much? Hogwash. God can carry you.

You're stronger than you think because God is nearer than you know.

Jesus touched wounds. He spoke words of hope. Lives were improved. Blessings were bestowed. There was a message in his miracles: "I am here. I care."

Had Jesus wanted just to make a case for his divinity, he could have materialized a flock of birds out of thin air and caused trees to uproot and float away. He could have turned creeks into waterfalls or rocks into bumblebees. Such deeds would have demonstrated his power. But Jesus wanted us to see more. He wanted to show us that there is a miracle-working God who loves, cares, and comes to our aid.

Do we not need this message today?

This book is a child of the quarantine. I completed it during the days of coronavirus. When I began writing it, some months ago, Covid-19 was unknown to most. Phrases like "social distancing" and "shelter in place" may have been found in manuals, but not in our street vocabulary. But that's all changed. As of this writing, millions of people are hunkered and bunkered in apartments, houses, huts, and cabins.

This crisis exacerbated an already rampant epidemic of isolation and depression. One study found that loneliness is as dangerous to one's health as smoking fifteen cigarettes a day. It can lead to dementia or Alzheimer's, heart disease, a weakened immune system, and a shorter life span.[1]

Administrators of one of the largest hospitals in America cite loneliness as a major reason for overcrowded emergency rooms. Parkland Hospital of Dallas, Texas, made this startling discovery as they were looking for ways to unclog the system. They analyzed data and compiled a list of high utilizers. They identified eighty patients who went to four emergency rooms 5,139 times in a twelve-month period, costing the system more than $14 million.

Once they identified the names of these repeat visitors, they commissioned teams to meet with them and determine the reason. Their conclusion? Loneliness. Poverty and food shortage were contributing factors, but the number one determinant was a sense of isolation. The ER provided attention, kindness, and care. Hence, the multiple return visits. They wanted to know that someone cares.[2]

Don't we all? The apostle John wanted us to know that Someone cares. He wanted us to believe, to set our weight fully upon the strength of this loving God.

When life feels depleted, does God care?

If I'm facing an onslaught of challenges, will he help?

When life grows dark and stormy, does he notice?

If I'm facing the fear of death, will he help me?

The answer in the life-giving miracles in the gospel of John is a resounding *yes*. Do you know these miracles? Do you believe in a Jesus who has not only power but a passionate love for the weak and wounded of the world? Do you think he cares enough about you to find you in the lonely waiting rooms, rehab centers, and convalescent homes of life?

I recently went on a walk with two of my best companions: my three-and-a-half-year-old granddaughter, Rosie, and my faithful, steadfast dog, Andy.

Andy loves to explore a dry riverbed near our house. And Rosie loves to follow right behind him. She thinks she can go wherever he goes. And when I offer to help her, she waves me away. She is a handful, this girl, kind of like her grandmother. So Andy led the way. Rosie scampered behind, and I tried to keep up.

Andy spotted a critter in a thicket of bushes and dashed into them. Rosie thought she could do the same. Andy ran straight through, but Rosie got stuck. The branches scratched her skin, and she began to cry.

"Papa Max! Will you help me?"

What did I do? I did what you would have done. I stepped into the thickets and extended my hands. She raised her arms and let me lift her out.

God will do the same for you. You are never alone, never without help, never without hope.

You and I long for Someone who will meet us in the midst of life's messes. We long to believe in a living, loving, miracle-working God who won't think twice about stepping into the thorny thickets of our world and lifting us out.

If this is your desire, take a good look at the words of John and the miracles of Christ and see if they don't achieve their desired goal: "That you may believe that Jesus is the Christ, the Son of God, and that believing you may have life in His name" (John 20:31).

CHAPTER 2

He Will Replenish What Life Has Taken

*H*e didn't look omniscient. He looked intelligent, with his horn-rimmed glasses, gray-flannelled suit, and stack of documents. He was smart, prepared, and every bit the statistician his profession demanded he be. Otherworldly and prophetic? Divine? Clairvoyant? I saw no halo. No attending angels. There was a glow to his face, but I chalked that up to the afternoon sun that fell through his office window.

"Let's see," he said, flipping through a binder of graphs and reports. "The two of you will live until . . ." He looked up long enough to say, "If you want to see for yourself, I'm on page seven." He paused while we caught up. My palms were beginning to moisten. Denalyn's eyes had widened. We'd been given dates before: due dates for our daughters, graduation dates from college, save-the-day dates for weddings. But a death date? Gave new meaning to the word *deadline*. Did we want to know his findings?

His full-time job was life insurance. Over the phone he'd told me, "I want to make certain you have what you need."

To do this, he needed two pieces of data: the amount of premium we were willing to pay and the number of our years remaining on earth. I could supply the first. He said he could supply the second. And now he was about to give it to us. "What if his date is this week?" I asked Denalyn. "Should I arrange for a guest speaker for the church?" She didn't smile. Neither did he.

He spoke with the casual tone of a hotel attendant reviewing reservation dates. "Mrs. Lucado, I've got you here with us until 2044. Mr. Lucado, your date of departure appears to be 2038."

Well, there it was. At least now we knew. I can't tell you much of anything else he said. I was transfixed on finally having my gravestone data. I knew the first number: 1955. I knew the next mark: a one-inch-long dash. (I measured it on a headstone once just out of curiosity.) Now I knew the second number: 2038.

This conversation occurred in 2018. I was down to, gulp, twenty years. I was three quarters of my way to crossing the Jordan. Armed with this new piece of data, I couldn't resist calculating my remaining resources:

- 168,192,000 breaths (Sounds like a lot. However, I used more than 2,000 writing the first draft of this chapter introduction.)
- 108,000 strokes of golf (or in my case the equivalent of ten games)
- 7,300 nights in bed with a sleeping beauty named Denalyn (a number that seems more than I deserve yet far less than I desire)

My list also included remaining presidential elections, Super Bowls, summer sunsets, and blooming-bluebonnet seasons.

The exercise reminded me of an oft-ignored truth: we are

running out. Running out of days, dates, and dances. The hourglass was irreversibly flipped the day we were born, and we've been depleting our resources ever since. We don't have what we had yesterday. Our spending is outpacing our deposits—a fact, I think, that explains the reasoning behind miracle number one in the ministry of Jesus. He was at a wedding. Mary, his mother, was present as well. She came to Christ with a problem. "They have no more wine" (John 2:3 NIV).

Had I been the angel on call that day, I would have intervened. I would have placed a wing between Mary and Jesus and reminded her about the mission of her Son. "He was not sent to the earth to handle such mundane, day-to-day tasks. We are saving his miraculous powers for cadaver calling, leper touching, and demon casting. No wine? Don't whine to Jesus."

But I was not the angel on call. And Mary enlisted the help of her Son to deal with the problem: empty wine ladles. Folks in first-century Palestine knew how to throw a party. None of this wedding and reception in one evening, no sir. Weddings lasted as long as seven days. Food and wine were expected to last just as long. So Mary was concerned when she saw the servants scraping the bottom of the wine barrel.

Fault poor planning by the wedding planner. Fault guests for guzzling more than their share. Fault Jesus for showing up with a troop of thirsty disciples. We are not told the reason for the shortage. But we are told how it was replenished. Mary presented the problem. Christ was reluctant. Mary deferred. Jesus reconsidered. He commanded. The servants obeyed and offered the sommelier what they could have sworn was water. He sipped, licked his lips, held the glass up to the light, and said something about their squirreling away the best wine for the farewell toasts. The servants escorted him across the room to see the six vats filled to the brim with fruit of the vine. The wineless wedding was suddenly wine flush. Mary smiled at her Son. Jesus raised a glass to his mother, and we are left with this message: our diminishing supplies, no matter how insignificant, matter to heaven.

I have a curious testimony to this truth. During one of my many less-than-sane seasons of life, I competed in Half Ironman Triathlons. The event consists of a 1.2-mile swim, a 56-mile bike ride, and a 13.1-mile run. Why was a fifty-year-old preacher participating in such endeavors? That's what my wife kept asking me. (Don't worry. I didn't wear a Speedo.)

During one of these races I prayed the oddest prayer of my life. Four of us traveled to Florida for the race. One of my friends had invited a competitor from Indiana to join us. All told, I knew these three participants. There were at least two hundred people whom I did not know, a fact that proved crucial to my story.

I finished the swim, if not dead last, at least nearly dead and almost last. I mounted my bike and began the three-hour trek. About a third of the way into the cycling portion, I reached into the pocket of my shirt to grab some GU. GU is a packet of easily eaten essential nutrients. Well, guess who forgot his GU? I was GU-less with a good thirty miles to go. One doesn't find any GU-selling convenience stores on the triathlon road.

Like you I've offered innumerable prayers in my life. I've prayed for the enfeebled as they died and for babies as they were born. I've prayed for broken hearts, homes, and bones. But I had never prayed for GU. Yet what was I to do? No GU means no go for an old guy like Max.

So I prayed. Between puffs and pedal strokes, I said, *Lord, this very well might be the only time in eternity you've heard this request. But here is my situation . . .*

Did GU fall from heaven? Well, sort of. The fellow from Indiana, the friend of my friend, one of the three people I knew out of the entire field, just "happened" to pedal up from behind me.

"Hey, Max, how's it going?" he asked.

"Well, I have a problem."

When he heard of my GU-lessness, he reached into the pocket of his biking shirt, pulled out three packs, and said, "I've got plenty!" He handed them to me and off he went.

You may very well be thinking, *Lucado, that is a lame example of answered prayer. I'm dealing with disease, debt, the threat of layoffs and letdowns, and you're talking about something as lightweight as GU in a race?*

That's precisely my point.

Indeed, I think that is Jesus' point. Of what import is a wineless wedding? Of all the needs of people on the planet, why would bone-dry wine vats matter? Simple. It mattered to Jesus because it mattered to Mary. If Jesus was willing to use divine clout to solve a social faux pas, how much more willing would he be to intervene on the weightier matters of life?

He wants you to know that you can take your needs—*all your needs*—to him. "Be anxious for nothing, but *in everything* by prayer and supplication, with thanksgiving, let your requests be made known to God" (Phil. 4:6, emphasis mine).

In everything—not just the big things—let your requests be made known.

Mary modeled this. She presented the need to Christ. "They

have no more wine." No fanfare. No drama mama. She knew the problem. She knew the provider. She connected the first with the second.

My kids did this. They had a way of telling me exactly what they needed when they needed it. I never received a phone call from one of them saying, "Please be a good father to me today, Dad." Or "I declare in the name of good parenting that you must respond to my deepest desires."

What I heard was "Can you pick me up?" "Can I get some money?" "May I spend the night with my friend?" "Will you help me with my homework?" "How did you become such a brilliant, wise, and handsome father?"

Okay, that last question might be a stretch. The point is, my daughters made specific requests. Did I recoil at the specificity? Was I insulted that they dared to tell me exactly what they needed? Of course not. I was their dad. It was their way of saying, "I depend on you." It falls to the father to heed the need and respond to the request of the child.

So I ask, Have you asked? Have you turned your deficit into a prayer? Jesus will tailor a response to your precise need. He is not a fast-food cook. He is an accomplished chef who prepares unique blessings for unique situations. When crowds of people came to Christ for healing, "*One by one* he placed his hands on them and healed them" (Luke 4:40 THE MESSAGE, emphasis mine).

Had Jesus chosen to do so, he could have proclaimed a cloud of healing blessings to fall upon the crowd. But he is not a one-size-fits-all Savior. He placed his hands on each one, individually, personally. Perceiving unique needs, he issued unique blessings.

A precise prayer gives Christ the opportunity to remove all doubt about his love and interest. Your problem becomes his pathway. The challenge you face becomes a canvas upon which Christ can demonstrate his finest work. So offer a simple prayer and entrust the problem to Christ.

Again Mary is our model. Look carefully at her back-and-forth with Jesus. In verse 3 she presents the need: "They have no more wine." In verse 4 Jesus is curiously unreceptive to the request, saying, "Dear woman, that's not our problem. My time has not yet come" (John 2:4 NLT).

Jesus apparently carried an appointment book. He had a time of revelation in mind, and that day in Cana was not the intended moment. He went to the wedding for the purpose of, well, going to the wedding. His to-do list that day did not contain the entry "Turn water into wine." Angels were not lining up to watch miracle number one because, as far as the Angelic Committee on Initial Miracles was concerned, the moment of the maiden miracle was scheduled for a later date.

Hence, Mary's petition was met with Jesus' hesitation.

You've heard the same. In your personal version of verse three, you explained your shortage: no more wine, time, vigor, or vision. Your needle was on empty; the tank had run dry; the bank account was showing a negative balance. You pleaded your case in verse 3. And then came verse 4. Silence. Quiet as a library at midnight. The reply did not come. No deficit-erasing deposit was made. When no answer comes, how does your verse 5 read?

Mary's could have read as follows:

"She stomped away in a huff."

"She declared that she no longer believed in her Son."

19

YOU ARE NEVER ALONE

"She said, 'If you loved me, you would answer my prayer.'"

"She said, 'All these years of doing your laundry and cooking your meals, and this is the thanks I get?'"

Mary's verse 5, however, reads like this: "His mother told the servants, 'Do whatever he tells you'" (John 2:5 NLT).

Translation? "Jesus is in charge. I'm not." "He runs the world. I don't." "He sees the future. I can't." "I trust Jesus. Whatever he tells you to do, do it." *Whatever* means whatever. Whatever he says, whatever he commands. Even if his "whatever" is a *nothing whatsoever*, do it.[1]

Mary made it clear: Christ was the king of the wedding. She might as well have placed a crown on his head and draped a robe on his shoulders. Thirty years of living with Jesus had taught her: Jesus knows what he is doing. She had faith, not that he would do exactly what she asked, but that he would do exactly what was right. Her belief in him gave her the strength to say, "If he says, yes, great. If he says, no, fine."

Something in the explicit faith of Mary caused Jesus to change his agenda.

> Standing nearby were six stone water jars, used for Jewish ceremonial washing. Each could hold twenty to thirty gallons. Jesus told the servants, "Fill the jars with water." When the jars had been filled, he said, "Now dip some out, and take it to the master of ceremonies." So the servants followed his instructions. (vv. 6–8 NLT)

Six water jars would create enough wine for—hang on to your hat—756 bottles of wine![2] Napa never knew such a harvest.

When the master of ceremonies tasted the water that was now wine, not knowing where it had come from (though, of course, the servants knew), he called the bridegroom over. "A host always serves the best wine first," he said. "Then, when everyone has had a lot to drink, he brings out the less expensive wine. But you have kept the best until now!" (vv. 9–10 NLT)

The miracle of Christ resulted in not just an abundance of wine, but the abundance of good wine.

Cooking wine would have sufficed. Convenience-store vintage would have met the expectations of the guests. A modest sip-with-pizza-on-a-Tuesday-night quaff would have been enough for Mary. But it was not enough for Jesus. Something powerful happens when we present our needs to him and trust him to do what is right: he is "able to do exceedingly abundantly above all that we ask or think" (Eph. 3:20).

It simply falls to us to believe—to believe that Jesus is king of each and every situation. So make your specific request, and trust him to do, not what you want, but what is best. Before you know it, you'll be raising a toast in honor of the One who hears your requests.

By the way, if you happen to be around in 2038, we'll let you know if our friend the life-span forecaster knew what he was doing.

CHAPTER 3

The Long Walk Between Offered and Answered Prayer

ill Irwin was not the first person ever to walk the Appalachian Trail. He was not the only individual to begin in Springer Mountain, Georgia, and conclude on Mount Katahdin, Maine. Other adventuresome souls have hiked the twenty-one hundred miles, endured the snow and heat and rain, slept on the ground, forded the streams, and shivered in the cold. Bill Irwin was not the first to accomplish this feat. But he was the first in this respect: he was blind when he did it.

He was fifty years old when, in 1990, he set out on the hike. A recovering alcoholic and committed Christian, he memorized 2 Corinthians 5:7 and made it his mantra: "For we walk by faith, not by sight." And that is what he did. He did not use maps, GPS, or a compass. It was just Irwin, his German shepherd, and the rugged terrain of the mountains. He estimated that he fell five thousand times,[1] which translates into an average of twenty times a day for eight months. He battled hypothermia, cracked his ribs, and skinned his hands and knees more times than he could count.[2]

But he made it. He made the long walk by faith and not by sight.

You are doing the same. Probably not on the trails of the Appalachians, but in the trials of life. You are walking, not on the path between Georgia and Maine. No, you are walking on a road even steeper and longer—the path between offered prayer and answered prayer. Between

- supplication and celebration
- bent knees and lifted hands
- tears of fear and tears of joy
- "Help me, Lord" and "Thank you, Lord"

Do you know the road? How it grows dark with doubts? How despair tags along as an uninvited companion? If you can relate, you'll find this story inspiring.

> As he traveled through Galilee, [Jesus] came to Cana, where he had turned the water into wine. There was a government official in nearby Capernaum whose son was very sick. When he heard that Jesus had come from Judea to Galilee, he went and begged Jesus to come to Capernaum to heal his son, who was about to die. (John 4:46–47 NLT)

The father was a man of high standing in the court of Herod. He was likely a Gentile. His modern-day counterpart might be a White House chief of staff or a presidential cabinet member. He held a position of status and oversaw a houseful of servants. But none of that mattered, for he had a son who was very sick. The son was a child, just a lad (John 4:49). No doubt the prominent aristocrat had summoned the finest physicians to help his boy. But no one could. His son still teetered on the brink of death. The dollar is not almighty. Neither rank nor riches can protect their possessors from disease and death. Certainly this father would have given both to see health return to his son.

He lived in Capernaum, a fishing village that served as the base of operations for Jesus. Peter had a home there. Jesus was known to speak in its synagogue. It's not hard to imagine a villager suggesting to the distraught father, "Ask the Nazarene to help your son. He has healing power." Jesus was well-known in Capernaum.

Jesus, however, was eighteen miles away in the village of Cana.[3]

The official set out. He gave his son's fevered brow a kiss and his anxious wife a promise and then headed northeast around the Sea of Galilee. The trek required food, planning, and a protection detail. A predawn departure would get him to Cana by sundown. If he left at midday, he would have spent the night in an inn or taken up lodging in a borrowed room. Either way, he could not enjoy the walk, stop to see the sights, or visit with anyone along the path. By the time he spotted Jesus in Cana, the official was no doubt weary and worried.

"He went and begged Jesus to come to Capernaum to heal his son, who was about to die" (John 4:47 NLT). Straightforward was this request. Urgent. He didn't mention his position, rank, or title. He didn't promise to make a financial contribution to the cause of Christ. He didn't imply he was worthy of divine assistance. He came to Christ as a desperate father. He *begged* Jesus to come to Capernaum. I envision the man on his knees, perhaps his face on the ground, imploring Jesus to return with him and heal his son. He not only had a request; he also had a plan of action. In his mind the two would walk side by side from Cana to Capernaum until they stood next to the dying boy.

The response of Christ surprises us. "Will you never believe in me unless you see miraculous signs and wonders?" (John 4:48 NLT).

Goodness gracious, I did not see this starchy question coming, did you? Only one miracle into John's gospel we hear Jesus saying, "Be careful." He waved a caution flag against a contingent faith, a faith that says *I will believe if . . .* or *I will believe when . . .*

What prompted this response? Perhaps the attitude of the villagers? They took note of the arriving official with an entourage in tow. They learned of his dying son and the plan to solicit the assistance of Jesus. They followed him, not out of concern for the boy, but out of fascination with the miracles. This was Cana, after all. Word of the water-to-wine miracle was on the streets. Perhaps they were hoping to see another display of power. "Come on, Christ," their presence suggested. "Show us what you can do."

Or perhaps Jesus saw contingent faith in the request of the father. The man not only asked for help, but he also told Jesus the way the help should be administered. "Come to Capernaum and heal my son." As a high-ranking official, he was accustomed to giving directives. He told subordinates what to do and how to do it. Was he doing the same with Jesus? Was his belief in Christ contingent upon the willingness of Christ to answer his prayer in a specific manner?

For whatever reason, Christ felt a warning was in order. In his first miracle Jesus rewarded the unconditional "whatever" faith of Mary. In this miracle he cautioned against the conditional faith of the people. Contingent faith is the faith of sidewalk chalk: it's beautiful when the sun shines, but it washes away when the rain falls.

The father did not reply to the caution. His heart was a dozen exits down the highway. He did not dispute the fact that some people demand miracles; he simply wanted to stay focused on the task at hand. "The official pleaded, 'Lord, please come now before my little boy dies'" (John 4:49 NLT).

His appeal could hardly be more genuine. His direction could hardly have been clearer. "Come now!"

And Jesus responded to it. "Then Jesus told him, 'Go back home. Your son will live!'" (v. 50 NLT).

Such good news! Or was it? Jesus answered the man's prayer—or did he? The nobleman had reason to rejoice, then again maybe not. The man asked Jesus to go with him to Capernaum. But Jesus told him, "Go back home. Your son will live."

This was the moment of truth for the father, the moment he set out on the longest walk. The prayer was offered in Cana. Would the prayer be answered in Capernaum? He did not know. He had to make a choice.

Perhaps the nobleman turned on a dime and floated home on the magic carpet of faith. Maybe he high-fived his way down the path, shouting, "My dying son will live!" Perhaps he slept like a baby that night and awoke with joy the next morning. The sun was shining, the sky was blue, and he skipped and whistled all the way home to Capernaum.

If so, he was a better man than I am. I would've gulped at Jesus' reply. I would've looked first at Christ, then at the road. First one way, then the next. "Are you sure, Jesus? Can't you walk with me, Jesus? My wife is a good cook. I told her I would bring you. Won't you please come with me?"

What if he arrived in Capernaum and the son wasn't better? What if the Messiah had moved on to another city before the father could find him again?

He made his choice. "The man took Jesus at his word and departed" (John 4:50 NIV). He believed in the spoken word of Christ.

> While the man was on his way, some of his servants met him with the news that his son was alive and well. He asked them when the boy had begun to get better, and they replied, "Yesterday afternoon at one o'clock his fever suddenly disappeared!" Then the father realized that that was the very time Jesus had told him, "Your son will live." And he and his entire household believed in Jesus. This was the second miraculous sign Jesus did in Galilee after coming from Judea. (vv. 51–54 NLT)

The good news from the servants was met with a good question from the father: What time did he get better? Reply: one o'clock. The very time Jesus had spoken the word.

Jesus had worked a long-distance healing. The miracle was not just in the life of the boy but in the saving faith of the entire household. Isn't that what Jesus desired? The physical healing was an unspeakable gift, for sure. But the boy eventually died. I know of no two-thousand-year-old person from Galilee. The life-giving miracle of Jesus was short-term. The faith-giving miracle of Jesus was eternal. The household believed in Jesus. This belief resulted in everlasting life.

What about you? Do you find yourself somewhere between Cana and Capernaum? Like the official you offered a heartfelt prayer. You begged Jesus for help. And like the official you didn't receive the answer in the way you wanted. Consequently, here you are, doing your best to place one foot in front of the other, walking the path of obedience.

This is the issue of not-yet-answered prayer. Or not-answered-in-the-way-I-asked prayer. When we request plan A and Christ responds with plan B, how should we react? How do we find the strength to do in our lives what Bill Irwin did in the Appalachians? How do we walk by faith when we are thus far blind to the solution?

May I approach this topic gently? Before I suggest an answer, may I tell you I am sorry we have to discuss the question? I'm sorry you have a yet-to-be-answered prayer. I'm sorry the job did not materialize, the spouse did not apologize, or the cancer chose to metastasize. I'm sorry you find yourself between Cana and Capernaum. Life has its share of dark, dank moments.

And Christ will not remove all the pain this side of heaven.

Did someone tell you otherwise? Did someone assure you that God permits only blue skies and rainbows and sunbeams? They misspoke. Read the Bible from the table of contents in the front to the maps in the back, and you will not find any promise of a pain-free life on this side of death.

But you will find this assurance: "Never will I leave you; never will I forsake you" (Heb. 13:5 NIV).

31

When the father reached Capernaum, he made this wonderful discovery: the presence and power of Jesus had gone ahead of him. He may have thought he was walking the road alone. Quite the contrary. Christ had supernaturally gone into the nobleman's residence and not only healed the son but also won the hearts of the entire household.

Was the father's prayer answered? By all means. It was answered in a manner greater than he had requested.

Yours will be as well. Perhaps the answer will come this side of heaven. Perhaps it awaits you on the other side. Either way, this story urges you and me to keep walking and believing in our God who is our "ever-present help in trouble" (Ps. 46:1 NIV). Don't you love that phrase?

Ever present. Not occasional or sporadic help. You'll never be put on hold or told to check back later. He's never too busy, preoccupied, or away on a prior engagement. God is . . .

Ever *present*. As near as your next breath. Closer than your own skin. "Where can I go from your Spirit? Where can I flee from your presence? If I go up to the heavens, you are there; if I make my bed in the depths, you are there" (Ps. 139:7–8 NIV). Rehab clinic? He is there. Prison cell? He is present. No boardroom is too superior. No brothel is too vulgar. No palace is too royal. No hovel is too common. "He is not far from any one of us" (Acts 17:27 NIV). He is present. And he is present to . . .

Help. Not hurt, harm, or hinder. He is here to help. That is the message of this miracle.

Do your days feel like a hike on an Appalachian Trail in the dead of winter? Is it all you can do to place one foot in front of the other? If so, I urge you to hang on! Hold on! Don't give up.

Help is here. It may not come in the manner you requested or as quickly as you desire, but it will come. Assume that something good is going to happen. The door to tomorrow is unlocked from the inside. Turn the knob and step out.

Some years ago my wife and I enjoyed a dinner in the Texas hill country home of Gerald Jones. You may not recognize the name Gerald Jones, but you've possibly heard his professional name: G. Harvey. He was one of the finest artists in America.

His house was a G. Harvey collector's dream. Wall after wall of original paintings. Frame after frame of perfection.

Behind the house was his studio, a workroom of unfinished paintings. Partially painted canvases. People with no heads. Mountains with no peaks. Now I'm far from an art connoisseur, but even I knew better than to point out these facts to the artist. How shortsighted it would have been for me to say, "Hey, Gerald, this tree is half-finished." Or "You forgot to paint legs on this horse."

The artist wasn't finished yet.

The Divine Artist isn't finished either. The earth is his studio. Every person on earth is one of his projects. Every event on earth is part of his great mural. He is not finished. "God began doing a good work in you, and I am sure he will continue it until it is finished when Jesus Christ comes again" (Phil. 1:6 NCV).

This life contains many walks from Cana to Capernaum, journeys between prayer offered and prayer answered. Jesus promised the boy's father a sure blessing at the end of the journey. He promises the same to us.

We will meet this father when we get to heaven. When we do, I'm going to ask him about that walk. I want to hear how he felt, to know what he thought. But most of all I want to thank him for inspiring this verse: "The man took Jesus at his word and departed" (John 4:50 NIV).

Do likewise. Set your compass on the polestar of God's promise, and place one weary foot in front of the other. Jesus has spoken. Let his word do what it was intended to do: lead you home.

Stand Up, Take Up, and Walk

imothy Cipriani's idea was simple. He would lower himself into the pizza restaurant from the ventilation duct, rob the cash register, and climb back out. The plan backfired. Either he had been eating too much pizza, or the ventilation duct was too narrow, because he got stuck. He dangled over a deep fryer, his legs hanging out of the ceiling, screaming for help. It took the police thirty minutes to free him.

It's terrible to be stuck. Just ask the eighteen people who rode a roller coaster in Anhui, China. Inclement weather at the amusement park brought the ride to a halt at the top of the loop, and eighteen passengers were suspended upside down for half an hour! All were rescued, but six had to go to the hospital.

How do you say, "I'm about to puke" in Mandarin?

And how do the people of Jiangsu Province say, "This stinks!"?

That was the opinion of the man who dropped his cell phone into a commode. Rescuers found him crouched over the toilet, his arm submerged up to his shoulder. Workers had to break the porcelain bowl to get him out.[1]

I hope the call was worth it.

Odds are you've never been stuck in a ventilation duct, on a roller coaster, or in a toilet, but you have been stuck. Lodged between a rock and a hard place, unable to escape. Mired in the mud of resentment, bogged down in debt, trapped in a dead-end career, up to your waist in the swamp of an unsolvable conflict. Stuck. Stuck with parents who won't listen or employees who won't change. Stuck with a harsh boss or a stubborn addiction.

Stuck.

The man near the pool of Bethesda didn't use the word *stuck*, but he could have. For thirty-eight years near the edge of a pool, it was just him, his mat, and his paralyzed body. And since no one would help him, help never came.

He was seriously, unquestionably, undeniably stuck.

Afterward Jesus returned to Jerusalem for one of the Jewish holy days. Inside the city, near the Sheep Gate, was the pool of Bethesda, with five covered porches. Crowds of sick people—blind, lame, or paralyzed—lay on the porches. One of the men lying there had been sick for thirty-eight years. (John 5:1–5 NLT)

They must have made a miserable sight: crowds of people—blind, lame, despondent, dejected, one after the other—awaiting their chance to be placed in the pool where healing waters bubbled up.[2]

The pool was large: 393 feet long, 164 feet wide, and 49 feet deep.[3] Five porticos were built to shelter the infirm from the sun. Like wounded soldiers on a battlefield, the frail and feeble collected near the pool.

We see such sights still today. The underfed refugees at the camps in Syria. The untreated sick on the streets of Bangladesh. The unnoticed orphans of China. Unattended indigents, unwelcomed immigrants—they still gather. In Central Park. At Metropolitan Hospital. In Joe's Bar and Grill. It's any collection of huddled masses characterized by pain and suffering.

Can you envision them?

And, more important, can you envision Jesus walking among them?

All the gospels' stories of help and healing invite us to embrace the wonderful promise: "Wherever [Jesus] went he healed people of every sort of illness. And what pity he felt for the crowds that came, because their problems were so great and they didn't know what to do or where to go for help" (Matt. 9:35–36 TLB).

Jesus was drawn to the hurting, and on that particular day he was drawn to the pool of Bethesda. What emotions did he feel as he surveyed the mass of misfortune? What thoughts did he have as he heard their appeals? Did they touch his robe as he walked past? Did he look into their faces? It was a sad, piteous sight. Yet Jesus walked into the midst of it.

His eyes landed upon the main character of this miracle, a man who "had been sick for thirty-eight years. When Jesus saw him and knew he had been ill for a long time, he asked him, 'Would you like to get well?' 'I can't, sir,' the sick man said, 'for I have no one to put me into the pool when the water bubbles up. Someone else always gets there ahead of me'" (John 5:5–7 NLT).

What an odd question to ask a sick person: Would you like to get well?

I've been visiting the sick since 1977. My first ministry assignment was a pastoral internship program that included regular rounds at hospitals in St. Louis, Missouri. Since that day I've spoken with hundreds, maybe thousands, of sick people: in churches, hospitals, eldercare homes, and hospice care units. I've prayed for migraines and measles. I've anointed with oil, held the hands of the dying, whispered prayers, raised my voice, knelt at bedsides, read Scripture, and stood with worried families. But I have never ever—not once—asked the infirmed, "Would you like to get well?"

Why would Jesus pose such a question? Our only clue is the phrase, "When Jesus saw him and knew he had been ill for a long time" (v. 6 NLT). The man was two years shy of four decades as an invalid. Thirty-eight years—almost the amount of time the Hebrews wandered in the desert. It was the duration of the condition that prompted Christ to ask, "Would you like to get well?"

What tone did Jesus use? Was he the compassionate shepherd? Did he ask the question with trembling voice and softness? Maybe.

But I don't think so. The phrase "when Jesus . . . knew he had been ill for a long time" makes me think otherwise. And the response of the man convinces me.

> "I can't, sir," the sick man said, "for I have no one to put me into the pool when the water bubbles up. Someone else always gets there ahead of me." (v. 7 NLT)

Really? *No one* will help you? Someone else *always* gets ahead of you? In thirty-eight years you couldn't inch your way down to the pool? Persuade someone to give you a hand? Thirty-eight years and absolutely no progress?

In that context Christ's question takes on a firm tone: *Do you want to get well?* Or do you like being sick? You have a good thing going here. Your tin cup collects enough coins to buy the beans and bacon. Not a bad gig. Besides, healing would be disruptive. Getting well means getting up, getting a job, and getting to work. Getting on with life. Do you really want to be healed?

That's the question Christ asked then. That's the question Christ asks all of us.

Do you want to get . . . sober? Solvent? Educated? Better? Do you want to get in shape? Over your past? Beyond your upbringing? Do you want to get stronger, healthier, happier? Would you like to leave Bethesda in the rearview mirror? Are you ready for a new day, a new way? Are you ready to get unstuck?

Ah, there it is. There's the word. That's the descriptor.

Unstuck.

Dislodged.

Pried loose.

Set free.

Let go.

Unshackled.

Unstuck.

Life feels stuck when life makes no progress. When you battle the same discouragement you faced a decade ago or struggle with the same fears you faced a year ago. When you wake up to the same hang-ups and habits. When Bethesda becomes a permanent mailing address. When you feel as though everyone gets to the pool before you and nobody wants to help you.

If that is you, then pay attention to the promise of this miracle. Jesus sees you. This Bethesda of your life? Others avoid you because of it. Jesus walks toward you in the midst of it. He has a new version of you waiting to happen. He says to you what he said to the man: "Stand up, pick up your mat, and walk!" (John 5:8 NLT).

Stand up. Do something. Take action. Write a letter. Apply for the job. Reach out to a counselor. Get help. Get radical. Stand up.

Pick up your mat. Make a clean break with the past. Clean out your liquor cabinet. Throw out the junky novels. Quit hanging with the bad crowd. Drop the boyfriend like a bad habit. Put porn filters on your phone and computer. Talk to a debt counselor.

And *walk.* Lace up your boots and hit the trail. Assume that something good is going to happen. Set your sights on a new destination, and begin the hike. Getting unstuck means getting excited about getting out.

Heed the invitation of this miracle: believe in the Jesus who believes in you. He believes that you can rise up, take up, and move on. You are stronger than you think. "'I know the plans I have for you,' declares the LORD, 'plans to prosper you and not to harm you, plans to give you hope and a future'" (Jer. 29:11 NIV).

He certainly gave a bright future to the Bethesda beggar. "And immediately the man was made well" (John 5:9). Jesus did nothing but speak, and the miracle was accomplished.

He did the same for Barbara Snyder in 1981. She hadn't walked in seven years. She had been a gymnast in her high school. But multiple sclerosis brought an end to that. She began bumping into doors and walls. The next sixteen years brought one crisis after another. She lost control of her bowels and bladder. She was nearly blind. She was given a tracheostomy, confined to a hospital bed in her home, and given six months to live. Harold Adolph performed twenty-five thousand surgeries in his career. He called her "one of the most hopelessly ill patients I ever saw."

But then came the command of Christ. A friend called the Moody Bible Christian radio station and requested prayers for her healing. Some 450 listeners wrote her church to say they were praying.

Barbara's aunt selected some of the letters and brought them to share with Barbara on pentecost Sunday 1981. As she was listening to the letters, Barbara heard a man's voice behind her. "My child, get up and walk!" There was no man in the room. One of her friends, noticing that Barbara appeared troubled, plugged the hole in her neck so Barbara could speak. "God just told me to get up and walk. I know he really did! Run and get my family. I want them here with us!"

They came. What happened next was described by one of her physicians, Dr. Thomas Marshall: "She literally jumped out of bed and removed her oxygen. She was standing on legs that had not supported her for years. Her vision was back . . . and she could move her feet and hands freely."

That night Barbara attended a worship service at Wheaton Wesleyan Church. When she walked down the center aisle, the people began to applaud, and then, as if prompted by a choir director, they began to sing "Amazing Grace."[4]

Christ did the work. Christ performed the miracle. Christ intervened. But, even so, Barbara had to believe. She had to get up and walk.

So do you. So do I.

When I presented this message to our church, a congregant

wrote me a letter. He recalled a Good Friday sermon in which I had shared the story of an elementary school teacher who instructed her students to list all the things they felt they could not do. The lists were placed in a box and buried in the schoolyard. By putting away the things they could not do, the students could focus on the things they could do.

The writer of the letter recalled that sermon. He related that his wife had died of cancer a few months prior to that Good Friday. On Easter weekend the grief was pulling him under. In one of her final acts, his wife had planted some poppy seeds in their lawn. They never grew.

He decided to put the ground that contained the poppy seeds to further use. He went home after the service and made a list of his "I can't"s. Things like "I can't get over Janelle's death," "I can't ever love again," and "I can't face my work." On Saturday morning he buried the list in the soil that contained the seeds. In his letter to me he wrote, "The burden was gone. I had an un-explainable feeling of PEACE/relief."

I'll let him tell you what happened next.

The next morning, Easter Sunday, I decided to go out to my burial site where I had buried my little box of "I can't"s. I wanted to meditate there and say a little prayer. As I approached the site, I was taken aback. There, swaying in the light breeze, was a single red poppy! I was awestruck![5]

God resurrected hope in the heart of the widower. He healed the body of Barbara Snyder.

What will God do for you? I cannot say. Those who claim they can predict the miracle are less than honest. God's help, while ever present, is ever specific. It is not ours to say what God will do. Our job is to believe he will do something. It simply falls to us to stand up, take up, and walk.

Jesus is serious about this command. When he found the just-healed man in the temple, he told him, "See, you have been made well. Sin no more, lest a worse thing come upon you" (John 5:14). To indulge in inertia is to sin! Stagnant, do-nothingness is deemed as a serious offense.

No more Bethesda for you. No more waking up and going to sleep in the same mess. God dismantled the neutral gear from your transmission. He is the God of forward motion, the God of tomorrow. He is ready to write a new chapter in your biography.

The man in John's story had waited thirty-eight years, but, God bless him, he wasn't about to wait another day. He could have. To be honest I thought he would have. Listening to his excuse, I would have thought he'd stay stuck forever. But something about the presence of Christ, the question of Christ, and the command of Christ convinced him not to wait another day.

Let's join him. Ask the Lord this question: What can I do today that will take me in the direction of a better tomorrow? Keep asking until you hear an answer. And once you hear it, do it. Stand up, take up, and walk.

We Can Solve This

The story I'm about to share qualifies me for admission into a diminishing population. Younger readers will quite possibly discount what I tell you as hyperbole. No one, they will reason, has been around that long. No one alive, they will surmise, still remembers those days. No one, they will tell their torn-jeans-wearing, tattoo-covered friends, is still alive who recalls the day that e-mail entered the world.

But, as God is my witness, I'm alive, I was there, and I remember.

The last decade of the twentieth century was just getting underway. Clinton still had some dark hair. Cars still had cassette players. And I embraced the misconception that e-mail was a passing fancy. It would go the way of Slinkies and Slip 'N Slides. (I misjudged those two as well.) Who in their right mind, I reasoned with my friends, would exchange handwritten letters for electronic mail?

What I didn't confess to them and am admitting publicly for the first time is that I was overwhelmed by the world of computers. It intimidated me. It was New York City, and I was a country hick.

It was Beethoven's Fifth, and I clunked playing "Chopsticks." It was the Pacific Ocean, and I was a minnow. Still I got thrown in.

I went to sleep one night in a world of sticky notes. I awoke the next morning in a paperless society that the avant-garde thinkers on our church staff had been dreaming of for months. "Just think," they would say, "move the cursor, click the mouse, and the message is sent."

My computer illiteracy was so severe I thought a cursor was a person who used foul language, a modem was something you flushed, and a mouse was a rodent you trapped. As far as I knew, logging on was the job of a lumberjack. And a monitor? We had one named Norman in our college dormitory.

How was I to know that *interface* was a computer term? I thought it was basketball trash talk to be used after a slam dunk. (InterFACE, baby!) Forgive me for lagging behind (or is it "logging behind"?), but I was intimidated. I was as plugged in as a toaster in an Amish kitchen. I didn't know where to start, how to act, or what questions to ask.

I guess you could say I was overwhelmed.

You know the word. You know the feeling. You know the paralyzing, deer-in-the-headlights fear that surfaces when the information is too much to learn, the change is too great to make, the decisions are too many to manage, the grief is too deep to survive, the mountain is too tall to climb, or the crowd is too numerous to feed.

At least that is what the disciples told Jesus.

After these things, Jesus went over to the other side of the Sea of Galilee (also called the Sea of Tiberias), and a huge crowd of people was following him because they had been seeing the signs (the significant things) he was doing with the sick. So Jesus went up into the mountain and was sitting there with his disciples. Now the Passover, the Festival of the Jewish people, was coming up. (John 6:1–4)[1]

John does us a favor by mentioning the proximity of the Passover. He gives us our calendar bearings. Passover was a springtime celebration. The winter chill of January and February was giving way to the warm breezes and wildflowers of March and April. This is the first of three Passovers mentioned in John's gospel. Jesus was just two springtimes away from his final Passover in the Upper Room.

For the Jews, Passover was a season of possibilities, a happy recollection of the exodus from Egyptian bondage that whet the appetite for a repeat performance. Would deliverance come in the form of the Nazarene miracle worker? Might he be their Moses and lead them to a promised land? They hoped so. They had seen the signs he had performed. They knew about the healings and the teachings. They followed him around the Sea of Galilee.

At a certain point Jesus realized that the multitude had nothing to eat. They had no more food in their sacks. They had no food trucks or stores in which to shop. These fifteen thousand-plus people (five thousand men plus women and children) were hungry.

"Where can we buy enough bread to feed all these people?" (Jesus was asking this to test Philip, because Jesus knew what he himself was going to do.) Philip responded, "Several thousand dollars' worth of bread wouldn't be enough to give even a tiny bite to all these people!" Then one of Jesus' other disciples, Andrew, the brother of Simon Peter, said to Jesus, "There is a boy here with five loaves of barley bread and two fish. Oh, but what are these things when there are all these people?" (vv. 5–9)[2]

Philip, a practical sort, looked out over the sea of faces. He heard the murmurs and imagined the grumbling stomachs and replied with no hesitation: "We ain't got what it takes to face this challenge. Our purse hasn't got the coins. Our budget hasn't got the moola. Our capacity hasn't got the ability. There are too many mouths and not enough dollars."

Note the thrice-repeated phrase "all these people."

1. Jesus' question: "Where can we buy enough bread to feed all these people?" (v. 5)
2. Philip's response: "Several thousand dollars' worth of bread wouldn't be enough to give even a tiny bite to all these people!" (v. 7)
3. Andrew's idea to start with the boy's lunch, but then: "What are these things [loaves and fishes] when there are all these people?" (v. 9)

Jesus acknowledged "all these people." Philip saw no help for "all these people." Andrew had an idea, but the suggestion wilted in the face (or faces) of "all these people."

What is your version of "all these people"?

It might be something as pedestrian as "all these diapers" or "all this homework" or "all these long days." Or it might be as disrupting as "all this dialysis," "all this depression," or "all these bills."

Whatever it is, the demand outstrips the supply, and you are left feeling as hopeless as Philip and as meager as Andrew.

We'd like to think the followers would respond with more faith. After all, they'd seen water turned into wine and a lame man walk. We'd like to see more spunk, more grit. More "We can't, but you can, Jesus!" But they and the silent others showed no spark. They counted the hungry people, the money in their bag, and the amount of bread and fish. They did not, however, count on Christ.

And he was standing right there! He could not have been nearer. They could see, hear, touch, maybe even smell him. Yet the idea of soliciting his help did not dawn on them.

Even so, Jesus went right to work.

Jesus said, "Please get the people seated." (There was a lot of grass there.) The people sat down; they numbered about five thousand men. So Jesus took the loaves, and when he had given thanks, he distributed them to those who were seated, and as much fish as they were wanting, too. So when they were satisfied, he said to his disciples, "Please gather up the leftovers so that nothing will be lost." Well, they gathered twelve whole baskets of leftovers from the overflow to those who had eaten the five barley loaves! (John 6:10–13)[3]

I envision the people sprawled out on the green grass, so satisfied that they needed a nap. Those who didn't sleep picked their teeth. No small amount of belching could be heard. Hungry bellies became happy bellies. There was so much food that twelve baskets of leftovers were gathered. (One souvenir for each doubting apostle?)

The impossible challenge of feeding "all these people" became the unforgettable miracle of all these people fed. The *Galilean Gazette* carried the headline "Banquet for Thousands!" and this lead sentence: "Christ did what no one imagined, just as he did at the wedding." Isn't that the lead sentence of the gospel message? What we cannot do, Christ does!

The problems we face are opportunities for Christ to prove this point.

If you see your troubles as nothing more than isolated hassles and hurts, you'll grow bitter and angry. But if you see your troubles as opportunities to trust God and his ability to multiply what you give him, then even the smallest incidents take on significance. Do you face fifteen thousand problems? Before you count your money, bread, or fish, and before you count yourself out, turn and look at the One standing next to you! Count first on Christ. He can help you do the impossible. You simply need to give him what you have and watch him work.

"Jesus took the loaves" (v. 11). He didn't have to use them. He could have turned the nearby bushes into fruit trees. He could have caused the Galilean sea to spew out an abundance of fish. He made manna fall for the Israelites. He could have done it again. Instead, he chose to use the single basket of the small boy.

What's in your basket?

All you have is a wimpy prayer? Give it. All you have is a meager skill? Use it. All you have is an apology? Offer it. All you have is strength for one step? Take it. It's not for you and me to tell Jesus our gift is too small. God can take a small thing and do a big thing. God used the whimper of baby Moses to move the heart of Pharaoh's daughter. He used the faulty memory of an ex-con to deliver Joseph from the prison and send him to the palace. He used David's sling and stone to overthrow the mighty Goliath. He used three nails and a crude cross to redeem humanity.[4] If God can turn a basket into a buffet with food to spare, don't you think he can do something with your five loaves and two fishes of faith?

Biddy Chambers did. Had she given up, no one would have criticized her. Had she walked away, no one would have thought less of her. Her God-given assignment was to partner with her husband in teaching the Bible.

They met in 1908, and by 1910 they were married, living in London, and busy about their dream of starting a Bible college. They purchased a large home and made rooms available for students and missionaries on furlough. Biddy's training was in stenography. She took careful notes of her husband's lectures and turned them into correspondence courses.

At the outbreak of World War I, he felt a call to minister to soldiers stationed in Egypt. He and Biddy and their two-and-a-half-year-old daughter moved to the Middle East, where he took a position as a chaplain. Their ministry continued. He taught, she transcribed. He lectured; she captured his messages. It was a perfect partnership.

Then came the setback. Her husband's complications from appendicitis rendered Biddy a widow. Her husband died at the age of forty-three. She buried him in Egypt and returned to London to face this question: How could she partner with her husband if her husband was gone? All dreams of a teaching ministry would need to be abandoned, right?

No. Biddy chose to give God her loaves and fishes. She set about the work of turning her husband's notes into pamphlets and mailing them to friends and acquaintances. Eventually they were compiled into a book. *My Utmost for His Highest* was published in 1927.[5]

No one could have predicted the impact that this volume would have upon its readers. Earliest devotees included Billy Graham, Bill Bright, and Henrietta Mears. Bill Wilson and Bob Smith, the founders of Alcoholics Anonymous, used to begin meetings with readings from its pages. George W. Bush turned to it for inspiration.[6] It has sold more than thirteen million copies and has been translated into more than thirty-five languages. The work of Oswald Chambers surely exceeded his fondest hopes. But it was the sincere faith of his wife, Biddy, that made the difference.

She gave what she had to Jesus, and with it Jesus fed, and feeds, the multitudes.

Let's follow her example.

The next time you feel overwhelmed remind yourself of the One who is standing next to you. You aren't alone. You aren't without help. What bewilders you does not bewilder him. Your uphill is downhill for him. He is not stumped by your problem. When you present your needs to him, he never, ever turns to the angels and says, "Well, it finally happened. I've been handed a code I cannot crack. The demand is too great, even for me."

You may feel outnumbered, but he does not. Give him what you have, offer thanks, and watch him go to work. Your list of blessings will be so long you'll need to buy a new hard drive for your computer so you can store it.

CHAPTER 6

I AM in the Storm with You

The stormiest season of my life occurred when I was twelve years of age. I was old enough for baseball, football, and bike riding. I was old enough to have a crush on a girl, own a bottle of English Leather cologne, and know the difference between a verb and an adverb. But I was not old enough to process what came my way that year: sexual molestation at the hands of an adult man.

He entered my world under the guise of a mentor. He befriended several families in our small town. I remember him as witty, charming, and generous. What I did not know—what no one knew—is that he had an eye for young boys.

He would have us over to his house for burgers. He would take us on drives in his truck. He took us hunting and hiking and offered to answer all the questions of life and love and girls. He owned magazines, the kind my father did not allow. And he would do, and make us do, things I will not repeat and cannot forget.

One weekend campout was especially perverse. He loaded five of us in a pickup camper and drove to a campground. Among his pack of tents and sleeping bags were a few bottles of whiskey. He drank his way through the weekend and worked his way through the tent of each boy.

He told us not to tell our parents, implying that we were to blame for his behavior. By swearing us to secrecy, he said he was keeping us from getting into trouble.

What a scoundrel.

I came home on Sunday afternoon feeling filthy and shame-ridden. I had missed a Communion service at church that morning. If ever I needed Communion, it was that day. So I staged my own Eucharist. I waited until Mom and Dad had gone to bed, and I went to the kitchen. I could not find any crackers, but I found some potatoes from the Sunday lunch. I could not locate any juice, so I used milk. I placed the potatoes on a saucer and poured the milk into a glass and celebrated the crucifixion of Christ and the redemption of my soul.

Can you let your imagination conjure up the image of the pajama-clad, redheaded, just-bathed, freckle-faced boy as he stands near the kitchen sink? He breaks the potato and sips the milk and receives the mercy of the Savior.

What the sacrament lacked in liturgy was made up in tenderness. Jesus met me in that moment. I sensed him: his love, his presence. Don't ask me how I knew he was near. I just did.[1]

Though the storm was severe, my Lord was near. And I learned a lesson I've never forgotten: Jesus comes in the midst of the torrent.

All of us will face our share of storms. No one gets through life scot-free. At one point or another the sky will darken, the winds will rage, and we will find ourselves in a modern-day version of the Galilean gusher.

When evening came, his disciples went down to the lake, where they got into a boat and set off across the lake for Capernaum. By now it was dark, and Jesus had not yet joined them. A strong wind was blowing and the waters grew rough. (John 6:16–18 NIV)

The hearts of the followers began to sink as their boat was certain to do. Their skin was soaked, throats hoarse, eyes wide. They searched the sky for a break in the clouds. They gripped the boat for fear of the waves. They screamed their prayers for help. But they heard nothing.

If only Jesus were with them in the boat. If only Jesus had told them to stay on the shore. But he was not in the boat, and he had told them to cross the water (Matt. 14:22). Consequently this moment had all the elements of a crisis.

The disciples were exhausted. They had to be! "They had rowed about three or four miles" (John 6:19 NIV). With a good current a boat can cover a mile every thirty minutes. But against the waves and the wind? They set out at sunset and were still rowing at three in the morning (Mark 6:48)! This was no carefree float trip on a lazy river. This was a backbreaking, boat-bouncing, terror-stirring push and pull of the oars. Don't you know that more than once they cried out to each other:

"I'm not going to last much longer!"

"We're not going to survive this!"

Look how Matthew described the condition of the storm. They were "in the middle of the sea, tossed by the waves, for the wind was contrary" (Matt. 14:24). They were too far from the shore, too long in the struggle, and too small against the waves.

And Jesus was nowhere to be seen. Have you ever encountered a dangerous, ominous, seemingly godforsaken storm?

Too far from the shore. Too far from a solution.

Too long in the struggle. Too long in the court system. Too long in the hospital. Too long without a good friend.

Too small against the waves. Too small and too alone.

The storm controlled the disciples.

Storms can dominate our lives as well. Just as we have no authority over the squalls of nature, we have no authority over the squalls of life. You may desire to save a marriage, but you have just one of two required votes. You may attempt to restore a rebellious child, but you can't be sure you'll succeed. You might pursue good health, but still face a pandemic. Storms overtake us. And it sometimes seems they will never end.

But then the unimaginable happens. "They saw Jesus approaching the boat, walking on the water; and they were frightened" (John 6:19 NIV).

The Bible narrative can move too quickly for our tastes. We want more description, more depiction, more explanation. This is one of those occasions. *Hold on, John. Before you hurry into the next sentence, describe this moment. People don't walk on water. They walk on rocks, dirt, and sand. But water? Was Jesus' hair blown back? Was he ankle-deep? Was his robe wet?* John gives no details, just this economical statement: "They saw Jesus . . . walking on the water."

That is all we need to know. Before Jesus stills the storms, he comes to us in the midst of our storms.

He says to us what he said to the disciples: "It is I; don't be afraid" (v. 20 NIV).

The literal translation of what Jesus said is "I AM; don't be afraid." I AM is God's name. If God had a calling card, it would contain this imprint: I AM. Ever since Moses saw the burning bush that refused to burn up, God has called himself "I AM" (Ex. 3:14). This is the title of steadiness and power. When we wonder if God is coming, he answers with his name: "I AM!" When we wonder if he is able, he declares, "I AM." When we see nothing but darkness, feel nothing but doubt, and wonder if God is near or aware, the welcome answer from Jesus is this: "I AM!"

Pause for a moment and let him tell you his name. Your greatest need is his presence. Yes, you want this storm to pass. Yes, you want the winds to still. But yes, yes, yes, you want to know, need to know, and must know that the great I AM is near.

The promise of Isaiah 43 is yours to cherish:

> "Don't be afraid, I've redeemed you.
> I've called your name. You're mine.
> When you're in over your head, I'll be there with you.
> When you're in rough waters, you will not go down. . . .
> . . . I am GOD, your personal God,
> The Holy of Israel, your Savior. . . .
> So don't be afraid: I'm with you."
>
> (ISA. 43:1–3, 5 THE MESSAGE)

We'd rather be spared the storm. Or if the storm comes, let it be mild and our deliverance quick. Let the application rejection lead to acceptance at a better college. Let the job dismissal come with a severance package and an offer of a better position. Let the marital strife turn quickly into romance.

Sometimes it does.

But when it doesn't, when we are thorax-deep in turbulence, Jesus wants us to know his name and hear him say, "I AM coming."

Such was the experience of the disciples. The moment they invited Christ into their boat was the moment they reached their destination. "So they gladly took him aboard, and at once the boat reached the shore they were making for" (John 6:21 PHILLIPS).

Follow the example of the disciples. Welcome Jesus into the midst of this turbulent time.

Don't let the storm turn you inward. Let it turn you upward.

On April 21, 2008, Katherine Wolf suffered a massive stroke. She didn't lose her life, but she lost her ability to walk, talk clearly, and care for herself. She went from being a California model to a wheelchair-bound patient. She's endured eleven surgeries and daily fights to regain her strength. More than once she has felt like giving up. One of those occasions occurred the day before Thanksgiving, seven months into her ordeal. Here is how she describes it:

> Despair washed over me as I watched Jay [her husband] and his sisters playing with James [their baby], lifting him in the air and running around with him in circles, laughing out loud, while I could barely even hold my head up because my neck wasn't strong enough yet.
>
> I found myself wondering, *Has God made a mistake? . . . I've gone from making lasagna in my little kitchen to being fed all meals through a tube in my stomach. . . . I've gone from wearing a cute outfit every day to wearing adult diapers and hospital gowns. . . . I should be in heaven right now. Then at least everyone's pain would eventually come to an end.*

Her loss could have hardly been more pronounced. From one moment to the next, her world was flipped upside down. Yet as her heart began to sink, God stepped in:

And then suddenly, before those thoughts had even fully landed in my head and heart, I felt a deep awakening of the Word of God, which I had known since I was a little girl. I could almost hear this rapid-fire succession of the truths of Scripture, like a dispatch from God Himself.

Katherine, you are not a mistake. I DON'T MAKE MISTAKES. I know better than you know. I'm God, and you're not. Remember that you were fearfully and wonderfully made in your mother's womb. . . .

There is purpose in all of this. . . .

Trust Me. I am working out EVERYTHING for your good. Don't doubt this truth just because you are in darkness now. What's true in the light is true in the dark.

I know you can't fight this. That doesn't matter. All you have to do is be still and let Me fight for you. I will complete the good work I began when I gave you new life. I will carry it on to completion. Believe that. My nature is to redeem and restore and strengthen. This terrible season will come to an end. You will suffer for a little while, and then I will carry you out of this.

. . . I have chosen you. Live a life worthy of this special calling you have received.

Something supernatural occurred in those moments as those truths hit me hard. God met me in the midst of the messiness of my life, and I felt fresh determination to press on and persevere. I suddenly felt extraordinary—in spite of my terrible pain. That moment changed everything for me. It was my epiphany of hope. I knew deep inside that my "earth suit" was only temporary. I would never lose heart in this situation because my soul was not what was wasting away. My body didn't work. That was all.[2]

Don't try to weather this storm alone. Row the boat and bail the water, but above all bid Christ to enter your sinking craft. Believe that you are never alone, that our miracle-working God sees you, cares about you, and will come to your aid. For all you know he may perform an immediate deliverance. You may reach your destination before you have a chance to wipe the rain off your face.

He is still the great I AM. When we find ourselves in the midst of Galilean waters with no shore in sight, he will come to us.

The next time you pray, *Is anyone coming to help me?* listen for the response of Jesus: *I AM with you in the storm.*

CHAPTER 7

He Gives Sight to the Blind

thought my sight was normal. I assumed the other fifth grad-ers saw what I saw when they looked at the blackboard: a patch of fuzzy lines. I didn't ask them if they could see the baseball when it left the pitcher's hand or the football when the kicker kicked it. I assumed they saw the ball when I did, at the last minute, with barely enough time to swing the bat or make the catch.

I had poor vision. But I didn't know it. I'd never known any-thing else.

Then my teacher called my mom. My mom called the optome-trist. The optometrist asked me to read some letters on a chart. The next thing I knew I was handed my first pair of glasses. Talk about a game changer! From one moment to the next, the fuzzy lines became clear. The baseball became big. The football was catchable.

I still remember the exhilaration of sudden sight. I would sit in Mrs. Collins's fifth grade classroom and lift and lower my glasses, moving from blurry to twenty-twenty, from distorted images to vivid faces. Suddenly I could see.

Christians talk like this. We, too, reflect on the joy of sudden sight. We love to sing the words to the old hymn: "Amazing grace! How sweet the sound that saved a wretch like me! I once was lost, but now am found; was blind, but now I see."[1] Blind. Blind to the purpose of life. Blind to the promise of eternal life. Blind to the provider of life. But now our sight is restored. We relate to the words of the was-blind beggar: "One thing I do know. I was blind but now I see!" (John 9:25 NIV).

His story is our story. Perhaps that's why John was in no hurry to tell it. He had thus far tilted toward conciseness. He needed only twelve verses to describe how water became wine. The healing at the pool of Bethesda required fifteen verses. Within fourteen verses the crowd was fed, and with only six the Savior walked on water. But when John placed pen to papyrus to describe the story of the blind man given sight, the apostle took his time. He dedicated a whopping forty-one verses to depicting how Jesus found, cured, and matured him.

Why? Among the explanations is this one. What Jesus did physically for the blind beggar, he desires to do spiritually for all people: restore our sight.

From heaven's viewpoint our earth is populated by sightless people. Blinded by ambition. Blinded by pride. Blinded by success. "Though seeing, they do not see" (Matt. 13:13 NIV). They do not see the meaning of life or the love of God. How else do we explain the confusion and chaos in the world? How else do we explain the constant threat of world war, plagues of hunger, and the holocaust of the unborn? How else do we explain the rising rate of suicide[2] and opioid addiction?[3] We have faster planes, smarter phones, and artificial intelligence, yet we are killing each other with guns and ourselves with drugs.

Billions of people simply cannot see. "The devil who rules this world has blinded the minds of those who do not believe. They cannot see the light of the Good News—the Good News about the glory of Christ, who is exactly like God" (2 Cor. 4:4 NCV). We need a spiritual ophthalmologist. We need Jesus to do for us what he did for the man on the side of the Jerusalem road.

"As [Jesus] went along, he saw a man blind from birth" (John 9:1 NIV). No one else saw him. The followers of Jesus may have observed the blind man. He may have entered their field of vision. But they did not *see* him.

The disciples saw only a theological case study. "His disciples asked him [Jesus], 'Rabbi, who sinned, this man or his parents, that he was born blind?'" (v. 2 NIV). The blind man, to them, provided an opportunity to talk spiritual philosophy. They didn't see a human being. They saw a topic of discussion.

Jesus, by contrast, saw a man who was blind from birth, a man who'd never seen a sunrise, who couldn't distinguish purple from pink. He dwelled in a dark world. Other men his age had learned a craft; he sat on the side of the road. Others had an income; he begged for money. Others had reason to hope; he had reason to despair.

Then Jesus *saw* him.

And Jesus sees you. The first lesson of this event is a welcome one. You and I aren't invisible. We aren't overlooked. We aren't dismissed. We may feel like a nameless beggar in the swarms of society, but this story—and dozens of others like it—assure us that

Jesus spots us on the side of the road. He takes the initiative. He makes the first move.

> "Neither this man nor his parents sinned," said Jesus, "but this happened so that the works of God might be displayed in him. As long as it is day, we must do the works of him who sent me. Night is coming, when no one can work. While I am in the world, I am the light of the world." After saying this, he spit on the ground, made some mud with the saliva, and put it on the man's eyes. (John 9:3–6 NIV)

Now there is something you don't expect to read in the Bible: Jesus spitting. A prayer would've seemed appropriate. Perhaps a "hallelujah!" But who expected to hear a guttural clearing of the throat? A heavenly spit into the dirt? The God who sent manna and fire dispatched a blob of saliva. And as calmly as a painter spackles a hole in the wall, Jesus streaked miracle mud on the man's eyes.

Of course, given the choice, we'd prefer that God would restore our sight with something more pleasant than mud in our eyes. Maybe a just-released covey of doves or an arching rainbow. To be sure, God grants such blessings. Other times he uses the less-than-pleasant. He initiates the miracle through "mud moments": layoffs, letdowns, and bouts of loneliness.

I can vouch for this unpleasant process of sight restoration. Denalyn and I moved to Brazil in 1983. She was twenty-eight years old. I was thirty. We were new to the ministry and riding high on missionary fervor. We were called to plant a church, a great church. We envisioned thousands of converts and decades of service. We were naive. Homesickness settled upon us like a cloud. I struggled to learn the language. Scantily clad bathers on Copacabana Beach gave new meaning to the phrase "culture shock." Brazilians were kind but less than interested in the ministry of green gringos whose use of past perfect tense was far from perfect.

Weeks. Months. One year. Two years. No growth in our church and then slow growth.

Our team of missionaries squabbled over and wrestled with strategies and direction. Buy a building? Start a broadcast? Street preach? Finally a breakthrough. A colleague felt convicted that we weren't preaching the gospel. (How could that be?) He urged us to meet, as missionaries, with open Bibles and open hearts and identify the core of the good news. So we did. For several consecutive Monday afternoons, we read and reread Scripture. I can't speak for the entire team, but I began to see clearly. The big news of the Bible? The message that was billboard worthy? That Jesus died for my sins and rose from the grave. Nothing more. Nothing less.

It was as if someone adjusted the lens on the telescope and I could see. Vividly. Clearly. Scales fell from my eyes.

We began to focus on the gospel message, and our little church began to grow. Even more, we began to grow. We grew in grace, love, and hope. During that season I wrote a book entitled *No Wonder They Call Him the Savior*. To this day, some three decades later, it is among the most widely received of my writings. It is nothing more than the day-to-day "reveal-ations" Jesus was giving me.

It all began with long bouts of fear, frustration, and failure. Mud in my eye.

Can you relate? If so, do not assume that Jesus is absent or oblivious to your struggle. Just the opposite. He is using it to reveal himself to you. He wants you to see him! Such was the case with the blind man.

Jesus told the blind man, "'Go, wash in the pool of Siloam' (which is translated, Sent)" (John 9:7). The water of Siloam was "sent" from an underground spring. John is making a subtle point. He has referred to Jesus as being sent by the Father no fewer than twenty times thus far in his gospel.[4] To see, we go to our Siloam, the "Sent One" of heaven, Jesus himself.

Access to Siloam involved the descent of three sets of stone-hewn steps, five steps each.[5] This was no casual stroll for anyone, much less a blind man. But he did it. He groped his way to the water. He leaned over the edge of the pool and began to splash his face and wash his eyes. As he did, he saw the water ripple and the sunlight sparkle on the pool's surface. He saw his fingers open and close. With another splash he could make out the forms of people who stood to either side. From one moment to the next, he could see.

The question is often asked, "What does a person need to know to become a follower of Christ?" This story provides an answer. The man knew nothing of the virgin birth or the Beatitudes. Did he know the cost of discipleship or the meaning of the Holy Spirit? No. He knew only this: a man called Jesus made clay, put it on his eyes, and told him to wash. He received sight, not because he deserved it, earned it, or found it. He received sight because he trusted and obeyed the One who was sent to "open eyes that are blind" (Isa. 42:7 NIV).

Nothing has changed. Jesus still finds blind people and restores their sight.

He promised that through his ministry "the blind shall see" (Luke 4:18 TLB).

The apostle Paul was sent to the Gentiles "to open their eyes and turn them from darkness to light, and from the power of Satan to God" (Acts 26:18 NIV).

Christ came to give light and sight.

Consider what Jesus is doing in the Muslim world. "More Muslims have become Christians in the last couple of decades than in the previous fourteen hundred years since Muhammad,"[6] and "about one out of every three Muslim-background believers has had a dream or vision prior to their salvation experience."[7]

For his book *The Case for Miracles,* author Lee Strobel interviewed Tom Doyle, a leading expert on contemporary dreams and visions experienced by Muslims. Doyle described a phenomenon of person after person seeing the same image: Jesus in a white robe, telling them he loves them, that he died for them, and urging them to follow him. This has been happening in Syria, Iran, and Iraq. It has happened so many times in Egypt that Christian outreach groups took out ads in the newspapers. The ads asked, "Have you seen the man in a white robe in your dreams? He has a message for you. Call this number."[8]

Doyle explains that 50 percent of Muslims around the world cannot read, so Jesus reaches them through dreams and visions. Eighty-six percent do not know a Christian, so Jesus goes to them directly.[9]

Jesus is in hot pursuit of the spiritually blind. They populate every pathway of every corner of the world. He finds them. And he touches them. He may use a vision, or the kindness of a friend, or the message of a sermon, or the splendor of creation. But believe this: he came to bring sight to the blind.

This task is reserved for Jesus. The Old Testament contains no stories of the blind being healed. The New Testament contains many, yet with only one exception each event of sight restoration was accomplished by Jesus. It is as if Jesus reserves the miracle of giving sight for himself.[10]

If you know the rest of the story of the formerly blind man, you know that he encountered resistance at every turn. His neighbors didn't believe him. The religious leaders excommunicated him, and his parents refused to defend him (John 9:8–9, 20–21, 34).

The poor guy went from seeing nothing to seeing nothing but resistance. Turns out he wasn't the only blind person in Jerusalem. The religious leaders called on him for an explanation.

They said, "What did he do to you? How did he open your eyes?"

"I've told you over and over and you haven't listened. Why do you want to hear it again? Are you so eager to become his disciples?"

With that they jumped all over him. "You might be a disciple of that man, but we're disciples of Moses. We know for sure that God spoke to Moses, but we have no idea where this man even comes from." (John 9:26–29 THE MESSAGE)

The leaders had the openness of a locked bank vault. A bona fide miracle had occurred, but did they seek to meet the One who caused it? Shouldn't the miracle have stirred at least some amazement? Some reason to pause? They saw nothing but themselves and their religion. Who were the blind ones in this story?

Charles Spurgeon said, "It is not our littleness that hinders Christ; but our bigness. It is not our weakness that hinders Christ; it is our strength. It is not our darkness that hinders Christ; it is our supposed light that holds back his hand."[11]

And because the leaders refused to see, "They cast him out" (John 9:34).

The was-blind man found himself kicked out of the temple with no one to defend him. "When Jesus heard what had happened, he found the man" (v. 35 NLT).

Christ was not about to leave the man unprotected. You can expect him to do the same for you. If you believe in him, he has given this pledge to you: "No one can steal [you] out of my hand" (John 10:28 NCV).

Others may disown you. Your family may reject you. The religious establishment may dismiss you. But Jesus? He will find you. He will guide you.

> When He [Jesus] had found him, He said to him, "Do you believe in the Son of God?"
>
> He answered and said, "Who is He, Lord, that I may believe in Him?"
>
> And Jesus said to him, "You have both seen Him and it is He who is talking with you."
>
> Then he said, "Lord, I believe!" And he worshiped Him. (John 9:35–38)

The story begins with a blind man seen by Christ. It ends with a was-blind man worshiping Christ. Is this not the desire of Jesus for us all?

Apart from Christ we are blind. We cannot see our purpose. We cannot see the future. We cannot see our way out of problems and pain. We cannot see Jesus. But he sees us, from head to foot. He knows everything about us.

When I was a fifth grader, the optometrist gave me a vision test. If God tested your spiritual vision, would you pass the test? Can you see the meaning of life? Have you caught a vision for eternity? Most of all, can you see God's great love for you? The hand you sense on your face is his. The voice you hear is his.

It is not his will that we grope blindly through life. He wants us to know why we are on earth and where we are going. Our vision matters to Jesus. He will do whatever it takes to help us see how to see.

CHAPTER 8

The Voice That Empties Graves

I spent a year in a cemetery one weekend. I arrived on a Friday and left on a Sunday, and the three days between my arrival and my departure felt like twelve months.

The visit to the graveyard was my big brother's idea. He was a nineteen-year-old college freshman. I was a sixteen-year-old high school junior. He had exchanged the hamlet of our upbringing for the thriving metropolis of Lubbock, Texas, the home of a hundred thousand residents, Texas Tech University, Lubbock Christian College, and the Resthaven Funeral Home and Cemetery.

The funeral home director made it a practice to hire college students as off-hour caretakers. It was a good gig for my brother. In exchange for a few nighttime patrols, Dee was given minimum-wage compensation, a flashlight, an upstairs efficiency apartment adjacent to the casket room, and a novel place to bring his girlfriend.

Turned out that she wouldn't step foot on the property. So he called me. (How bored do you have to be before you invite your baby brother to spend a weekend with you?)

Sounded like fun, until I got there. Then I saw black hearses parked outside. I saw unchiseled headstones in the storage yard and caskets for sale in the casket room. I saw the closet where gravediggers stored their equipment and the sign on the door that read Embalming. Dee thought the place was cool. I thought it was creepy. I arrived at five on Friday and was ready to leave at five fifteen.

You've noticed, I'm sure, that funeral homes aren't really homes. Though the grass is manicured, though the facilities are nice, who lingers, loiters, or lives in a cemetery? The sign may read Perpetual Rest or Peace in the Valley, but we seek rest and peace elsewhere. We go to a cemetery to pay respects and bid farewell. But picnic, play ball, or toss a Frisbee? No way. We depart as soon as possible.

Each headstone reminds us: life is but a dash between two dates. Each memorial service retells us: our time is coming. The grave is a grave thought indeed. We do all we can to delay our appointment with it. We exercise more, eat a bit healthier, buy cream for the wrinkles or vitamins for the body. But in the end there is an end . . . to this life.

Gee, Max, how kind of you to remind me. Your words are just what I needed to put a spring in my step.

You're right. We don't discuss graveyards to brighten our day. Cemeteries aren't typically known for their inspiration. But an exception was found in a graveyard near Bethany. And that one exception is exceptional.

A man named Lazarus was sick. He lived in Bethany with his sisters, Mary and Martha. This is the Mary who later poured the expensive perfume on the Lord's feet and wiped them with her hair. Her brother, Lazarus, was sick. So the two sisters sent a message to Jesus telling him, "Lord, your dear friend is very sick." (John 11:1–3 NLT)

John weighted the opening words of the chapter with reality: "A man named Lazarus was sick." Your journal might reveal a comparable statement. "A woman named Judy was tired." "A father named Tom was confused." "A youngster named Sophia was sad."

Lazarus was a real person with a real problem. He was sick; his body ached; his fever raged; his stomach churned. But he had something going for him. Or, better stated, he had *Someone* going for him. He had a friend named Jesus, the water-to-wine, stormy-sea-to-calm-waters, picnic-basket-to-buffet Jesus. Others were fans of Christ. Lazarus was friends with him.

So the sisters of Lazarus sent Jesus a not-too-subtle message: "Lord, your dear friend is very sick."

They appealed to the love of Jesus and stated their problem. They did not tell him how to respond. No presumption. No overreaching or underreacting. They simply wrapped their concern in a sentence and left it with Jesus. A lesson for us perhaps?

Christ responded to the crisis of health with a promise of help. "But when Jesus heard about it he said, 'Lazarus's sickness will not end in death. No, it happened for the glory of God so that the Son of God will receive glory from this'" (John 11:4 NLT).

It would have been easy to misunderstand this promise. The listener could be forgiven for hearing "Lazarus will not face death or endure death." But Jesus made a different promise: "This sickness will not end in death." Lazarus, we learn, will find himself in the valley of death, but he will not stay there.

The messenger surely hurried back to Bethany and told the family to take heart and have hope.

Yet "he [Jesus] stayed where he was for the next two days" (v. 6 NLT).

The crisis of health was exacerbated by the crisis of delay. How many times did Lazarus ask his sisters, "Is Jesus here yet?" How many times did they mop his fevered brow and then look for Jesus' coming? Did they not assure one another, "Any minute now Jesus will arrive"?

But days came and went. No Jesus. Lazarus began to fade. No Jesus. Lazarus died. No Jesus.

"When Jesus arrived at Bethany, he was told that Lazarus had already been in his grave for four days" (v. 17 NLT). "Israel's rabbinic faith taught that for three days a soul lingered about a body, but on the fourth day it left permanently."[1] Jesus was a day late, or so it seemed.

The sisters thought he was. "When Martha got word that Jesus was coming, she went to meet him. But Mary stayed in the house. Martha said to Jesus, 'Lord, if only you had been here, my brother would not have died'" (vv. 20–21 NLT).

She was disappointed in Jesus. "If only you had been here." Christ did not meet her expectations. By the time Jesus arrived Lazarus had been dead for the better part of a week. In our day his body would have been embalmed or cremated, the obituary would have been printed, the burial plot purchased, and the funeral at least planned, if not completed.

I know this to be true because I've planned many funerals.

And in more memorials than I can count, I've told the Lazarus story. I've even dared to stand near the casket, look into the faces of modern-day Marthas, Marys, Matthews, and Michaels and say, "Maybe you, like Martha, are disappointed. You told Jesus about the sickness. You waited at the hospital bed. You kept vigil in the convalescent room. You told him that the one he loved was sick, sicker, dying. And now death has come. And some of you find yourselves, like Mary, too bereaved to speak. Others, like Martha, too bewildered to be silent. Would you be willing to imitate the faith of Martha?"

Look again at her words: "Lord, *if only* you had been here, my brother would not have died. But *even now I know* that God will give you whatever you ask" (vv. 21–22 NLT, emphasis mine). How much time do you suppose passed between the "if only" of verse 21 and the "even now I know" of verse 22? What caused the change in her tone? Did she see something in the expression of Christ? Did she remember a promise from the past? Did his hand brush away her tear? Did his confidence calm her fear? Something moved Martha from complaint to confession.

Jesus responded with a death-defying promise: "Jesus told her, 'Your brother will rise again.' 'Yes,' Martha said, 'he will rise when everyone else rises, at the last day.' Jesus told her, 'I am the resurrection and the life. Anyone who believes in me will live, even after dying. . . . Do you believe this?'" (vv. 23–26 NLT).

The moment drips with drama.

Consider to whom Jesus asked this question: a bereaved, heartbroken sister.

Consider where Jesus stood as he asked this question: within the vicinity, perhaps in the center, of a cemetery.

Consider when Jesus asked this question: four days too late. Lazarus, his friend, was four days dead, four days gone, four days buried.

Martha has had plenty of time to give up on Jesus. Yet now this Jesus has the audacity to pull rank over death and ask, "Do you believe this, Martha? Do you believe that I am Lord of all, even of the cemetery?"

Maybe she answered with a lilt in her voice, with the conviction of a triumphant angel, fists pumping the air and face radiant with hope. Give her reply a dozen exclamation marks if you want, but I don't. I hear a pause, a swallow. I hear a meek "Yes, Lord, . . . I have always believed you are the Messiah, the Son of God, the one who has come into the world from God" (v. 27 NLT).

Martha wasn't ready to say Jesus could raise the dead. Even so, she gave him a triple tribute: "the Messiah," "the Son of God," and "the one who has come into the world." She mustered a mustard-seed confession. That was enough for Jesus.

Martha fetched her sister. Mary saw Christ and wept. And "when Jesus saw her weeping and saw the other people wailing with her, a deep anger welled up within him, and he was deeply troubled. 'Where have you put him?' he asked them. They told him, 'Lord, come and see.' Then Jesus wept" (vv. 33–35 NLT).

What caused Jesus to weep? Did he cry at the death of his friend? Or the impact death had on his friends? Did he weep out of sorrow? Or anger? Was it the fact of the grave or its control over people that broke his heart?

It must have been the latter because a determined, not despondent, Jesus took charge. Jesus told them to roll the stone away. Martha hesitated. Who wouldn't? He insisted. She complied. Then came the command, no doubt the only command ever made to a cadaver. Jesus, prone as he was to thank God for impossible situations, offered a prayer of gratitude, and "then Jesus shouted, 'Lazarus, come out!' And the dead man came out, his hands and feet bound in graveclothes, his face wrapped in a headcloth. Jesus told them, 'Unwrap him and let him go!'" (vv. 43–44 NLT).

Oh, I wish you were reading that paragraph for the first time. Your eyes would widen to the size of saucers. You would lower this book and look into heaven. "Did you really? Did you really shout in a cemetery for a dead man to come out?"

He did! Jesus issued a command, not an invitation; an imperative, not an idea; a summons, not a suggestion. Jesus . . .

- "cried with a loud voice" (NRSV),
- "roared with a great voice,"[2]
- "shouted as loudly as he could" (GOD'S WORD).

The Resurrection and the Life issued a command into the cavern of death. Somewhere in heaven an angel heard the familiar voice of the Shepherd and smiled. Somewhere in hell the fallen angel mumbled, "Oh no."

"Lazarus, come out!" The sound of the voice of God echoed off the grotto walls until the words found their way into the corner of paradise where sat a healthy, happy Lazarus in a corner café, sipping a latte with Moses, hearing firsthand accounts of the exodus.

"Lazarus!"

He heard his name and looked at Moses. The patriarch shrugged. "You have to go, friend."

Lazarus did not want to go back to earth. Of that I'm certain. But when Jesus commands, his disciples obey. Of that Lazarus was certain. So his spirit descended from the heavens and down through the skies until he reached the Bethany Burial Garden. He reentered and reanimated his body. He stood up and lumbered toward the mouth of the tomb.

"'Now unbind him,' Jesus told them, 'and let him go home'" (v. 44 PHILLIPS).

"Don't miss the message of this miracle," I love to say at funerals, although careful not to get too animated, because, after all, it is a memorial service. Still, I indulge in some excitement. "You are never alone. Jesus meets us in the cemeteries of life. Whether we are there to say goodbye or there to be buried, we can count on the presence of God."

He is "Lord both of the dead and of the living" (Rom. 14:9 ESV). An encore is scheduled. Lazarus was but a warm-up. Jesus will someday shout, and the ingathering of saints will begin. Graveyards, ocean depths, battlefields, burned buildings, and every other resting place of the deceased will give up the dead in whatever condition they might be found. They will be recomposed, resurrected, and re-presented in the presence of Christ.

Salvation of the saints is not merely the redemption of souls but also the recollection of souls and bodies.

It is plain to anyone with eyes to see that at the present time all created life groans in a sort of universal travail. And it is plain, too, that we who have a foretaste of the Spirit are in a state of

painful tension, while we wait for that *redemption of our bodies.*
(Rom. 8:22–23 PHILLIPS, emphasis mine)

We await, not a redemption *from* our bodies, but the redemption *of* our bodies. The totality of our humanness will be reclaimed. We are "fearfully and wonderfully made" (Ps. 139:14) yet frail and temporary "like the flower of the field" (Isa. 40:6). Our frailty is short lived. As joint heirs with Christ, we will enjoy a deliverance identical to his. "We will certainly also be united with him in a resurrection like his" (Rom. 6:5 NIV).

Do you believe this? Jesus' question to Martha is his question to you.

Death is the great equalizer. What do the billionaire and the peasant have in common? Both will die. We all will. But not all will face death in the same manner. Let the story of the resurrected Lazarus remind you: Jesus' authority extends over even the cemetery.

Do *you* believe this? Not your church, your family, your parents, or society, but you. The question is personal. What's more, it is precise.

Do you believe *this*? This claim Christ makes about his deity and about your destiny? Jesus is Lord over the cemetery. His voice can empty a grave. And you are destined for a Lazarus moment. Do you believe *this*?

George H. W. Bush did. Few people have led a more vibrant life than the forty-first president of the United States. Fighter pilot. Congressman. Ambassador. CIA director. Vice president for eight years. President for four. He had access to power and influence like few people in history. Yet none of that mattered on November

29, 2018. His ninety-four-year-old body was frail. In what would turn out to be his next-to-final day on earth, he received his good friend James Baker.

Baker called him "Jefe," Spanish for "Boss." Bush called Baker "Bake." The two often went out for lunch together. Baker would enter the house and say, "Where are we going today, Jefe?" But on this day the former president asked the question before Baker could. "Where are we going today, Bake?" His longtime friend replied, "Well, Jefe, we are going to heaven." To which Bush replied, "Good . . . because that is where I want to go."

Wanting to make sure I had the details of this story correct, I texted Russ Levenson, the pastor of the Bush family in Houston. He added this note: "In his final days we spoke often about heaven. He never asked, 'Will I go?' or 'Is there a heaven?' He just wanted to know what it was like."[3]

President Bush led a stellar life. But in the end it was not his accomplishments that mattered. It was his decision to trust the accomplishment of a Jewish rabbi.

I still don't linger in cemeteries. My weekend at the Resthaven Funeral Home didn't leave me longing to return. Offer me a chance to make a funeral home my home, and I'll pass, thank you very much.

I do what most visitors to a cemetery do. I pay my respects, attend the memorial service, and leave. I do indulge one imagining, however. I pause and look around the cemetery and envision the fulfillment of this promise:

For the Lord himself will come down from heaven with a commanding shout, with the voice of the archangel, and with the trumpet call of God. First, the believers who have died will rise from their graves. Then, together with them, we who are still alive and remain on the earth will be caught up in the clouds to meet the Lord in the air. Then we will be with the Lord forever. So encourage each other with these words. (1 Thess. 4:16–18 NLT)

CHAPTER 9

Paid in Full

A sk those who watched Kayla Montgomery run, and they will tell you that Kayla was a steady runner, a sturdy runner. Whip thin and determined, she was one of the fastest long-distance racers in the country. Trained eyes took note of her stride and strong finish. Her performance on the high school squad in Winston-Salem, North Carolina, caught the attention of coaches, competitors, and colleges. She set distance records, won state titles, competed in nationals, and eventually landed an athletic scholarship to Lipscomb University in Nashville, Tennessee.

Had you watched her run, you would have been impressed.

Here is what you never would have imagined: she ran with no feeling in her legs. She was diagnosed with multiple sclerosis at the age of fifteen. The disease is an autoimmune disorder that strictly targets the myelin sheath of the nerves, affecting the brain and spine. Heat sensitivity is one of many possible symptoms of MS. When Kayla overheats, her MS symptoms flare up, leaving her numb from the waist down.

Still she wanted to run. She told her coach, "I want to run, and I want to run fast." And she did. At one time she was ranked twenty-first in the nation.

The numbness would begin to set in after the first-mile marker. After that she relied on the momentum, as if on autopilot, to keep moving. Running was doable. Stopping? That was another story. She would cross the finish line with no ability to decelerate.

For this she depended entirely on one man, her coach. He was a fixture at the races, shouting, encouraging, and prodding, but his greatest contribution was catching. He caught Kayla. He would stand at the finish line awaiting her. She ran right into his arms. She didn't slow down. He didn't move. It was no small collision. When he finally was able to halt her forward progress, he would lift her five-feet-one-inch frame in a heap and carry her off the track.

Over and over she could be heard saying, "My legs! My legs! Where'd they go? Please help me. Please help me."

Over and over the coach assured, "It's okay. I got you. I got you."

He would carry her to a safe spot and give her water and ice. Gradually her body temperature would lower, and the feeling in her legs would return.[1]

They had an agreement. She did the running; he did the catching. If he was not present to catch her, she would eventually crash into the next obstacle. But she never crashed, because he was ever present.

This was his pledge to her.

This is God's pledge to us.

Your finish line is drawing near. Forgive the unsolicited reminder, but every stride and step bring you closer to your final one. Each beat of the heart is the click of a countdown clock. Your breaths are numbered. Your days are measured. No matter how well you run this race, you will not run it forever.

You're going to need some help. Your strength expires at the finish line. The skill with which you have run? The competence with which you have competed? The determination that carried you around the track? Your training? Experience and accomplishments? They matter not at all once you cross the line.

You're going to need someone to catch you.

Jesus has promised to be that Someone. He will not abandon you in your final moments. This is his promise. And this is the message of the cross.

> Later, knowing that everything had now been finished, and so that Scripture would be fulfilled, Jesus said, "I am thirsty." A jar of wine vinegar was there, so they soaked a sponge in it, put the sponge on a stalk of the hyssop plant, and lifted it to Jesus' lips. When he had received the drink, Jesus said, "It is finished." With that, he bowed his head and gave up his spirit. (John 19:28–30 NIV)

Does the crucifixion qualify as a miracle? By all means. It embodies every feature of the other miracles in John's gospel. In the miracle of the atonement, water didn't become wine, but sinners became saints. On Calvary Jesus didn't heal a servant with a proclamation; he healed all generations with an affirmation. On Good Friday Jesus didn't tell a lame man to walk; he invited us all to dance.

With a single proclamation Jesus fed more than a crowd, stilled more than a storm, and gave sight to more than one man. His command at the Bethany cemetery was enough to call Lazarus from the grave. His announcement on Calvary was sufficient to save all who believe in him from eternal death.

The announcement? *Tetelestai.* "It is finished" (John 19:30 NIV).

Remove your hat. Take off your shoes. Silence all chatter and lower your eyes. This is a holy word, a sacred moment.

The artist steps back from the canvas and lowers his brush.

It is finished.

The poet reads his sonnet one final time and then places his pen on the desk.

It is finished.

The farmer gazes out over the just-harvested field, removes his hat, and wipes his brow.

It is finished.

Jesus opens his swollen eyes and looks toward the heavens. His burning lungs issue enough air for him to announce, "It is finished."

Do you recall how his work began? When he was twelve years of age, Jesus went missing in Jerusalem. After three days his parents found him in the temple, talking with the rabbis. "Why did you seek Me? Did you not know that I must be about My Father's business?" (Luke 2:49). Even as a boy, Jesus had a sense of the family business, the work of redemption. His first recorded words marked its beginning. One of his final words signaled its completion.

Indeed, the Greek word *tetelestai* carries overtones of a business term. It was used to signify "paid in full" on debts such as levies or a tribute. The apostle Paul used a version of this word (Rom. 13:6) when he told us to "pay taxes." The root *teleó* appears in verse 24 of Matthew 17: "Does your teacher pay the Temple tax?" (NCV). The term indicates a finalized transaction.

Christ's word on the cross declares the same. "For by one offering He [Christ] has perfected forever those who are being sanctified" (Heb. 10:14). No further offering is needed. Heaven awaits no additional sacrifice. The work of Christ on the cross satisfied the demands of the eternal tribune. If that doesn't qualify as a miracle, what does?

"And bowing His head, He gave up His spirit" (John 19:30). His head did not fall forward or slump. He *bowed* his head. He *lowered* his head. Jesus was no exhausted, swooning sufferer. "No one takes it [my life] from me," he had promised, "but I lay it down of my own accord" (John 10:18 NIV).

The man on the center cross commanded center stage. He was sovereign, even in—especially in—death. The family business to which he referred as a boy was finished some twenty-one years later and half a mile to the west, on the hill of Golgotha.

Exactly what was finished? The teaching of Christ? No, he would go on to teach in a resurrected body for forty more days. The leading of the saints? No, he continues, with the Holy Spirit, to guide his church. Was the healing ministry of Jesus complete? By no means. In concert with the Holy Spirit and the compassion of the Father, Jesus still heals. But there is one task to which he no longer needs to tend: the redemption of humankind.

"For our sake he [God] made him [Christ] to be sin who knew no sin, so that in him we might become the righteousness of God" (2 Cor. 5:21 RSV). This verse describes the supernatural transfer of our sin to Christ and his righteousness to us. Jesus, God's sinless Son, absorbed in himself our sinful state. And we, his rebellious creation, can receive the goodness of Jesus.

In an earlier verse Paul wrote, "in Christ God was reconciling the world to himself, not counting their trespasses against them" (2 Cor. 5:19 RSV). God does not count our sins against us!

Instead, he counts them against Christ. Jesus voluntarily accepted liability for your sins. He generously offers to you the reward of his perfection.

After Jesus "had offered one sacrifice for sins forever, [he] sat down at the right hand of God" (Heb. 10:12). Of course Jesus sat down. All that needed to be done had been done. All that needed to be paid had been paid.

Christ has paid for you.

I heard a similar phrase recently in a drive-through Starbucks line. I placed my order and then waited until the occupants of the car ahead of mine made their purchases and drove on. When my turn came, I pulled up to the window and offered the attendant my cash. She waved it away. "The folks in the car ahead of you paid for your drink. They said they recognized you from their church and wanted to cover your coffee."

Who those people are, I do not know, but I know they are Christians of the highest caliber. And they set a sterling example for others to follow. "They left more than enough," the attendant continued as she held up a twenty-dollar bill. Since my drink cost less than five dollars, I did what any good preacher would do. I looked in my rearview mirror, then looked back at the attendant, and ordered something to eat.

What I did not do was refuse the gift. What I did not do was tell the attendant I needed no assistance. What I did not do was dismiss the act of grace. I simply and gratefully received it.

I so hope you will do the same.

Receive this, the great miracle of mercy. Let the grace of God flow over you like a cleansing cascade, flushing out all dregs of guilt and shame. Nothing separates you from God. Your conscience may accuse you, but God accepts you. Others may dredge up your past, but God doesn't. As far as he is concerned, the work is once-and-for-all-time finished.

I took a break from writing this book to go to the beach with our family. Rosie, grandchild number one, was three-and-a-half years old and had never seen the ocean. We all wondered how she would respond to the sight. When she saw the waves and heard the roar of the water, she watched and listened and then finally asked, "When does it turn off?"

It doesn't, sweetie.

We ask the same about God's grace. Surely it will dry up and stop flowing, right? Wrong. Surely we will exhaust his goodness, won't we? Never. We will at some point write one too many checks on his mercy and love, correct? Incorrect.

> He doesn't treat us as our sins deserve,
>> nor pay us back in full for our wrongs.
> As high as heaven is over the earth,
>> so strong is his love to those who fear him.
> And as far as sunrise is from sunset,
>> he has separated us from our sins.
> As parents feel for their children,
>> GOD feels for those who fear him.
>
> (Ps. 103:10–13 THE MESSAGE)

Keep running the race. And as you run, be assured. A Friend is waiting for you at the finish line. When you cross it, he'll catch you in his arms. Don't be surprised if he says again what he said then: "It is finished."

CHAPTER 10

He Saw and Believed

t might surprise you to know how often I have wrestled with doubts. You might defrock me if you knew how many times I have thought something like *Is this truly true?* To believe that God descended to earth. To believe that God became a baby, wore diapers, and suckled a mama's milk. To think a married couple had a baby before having sex. To think that a speck of dustiness called Nazareth served for three decades as the hometown of the Son of God. To think that God in the form of a prune-faced infant took a first breath, as a round-faced toddler took a first step, as a smooth-faced child took a first glance at a sunrise, as a pimply faced teenager took a first look at a pretty girl, as a slender-faced young man took a shot at reciting the Torah, *his* Torah, and as a bearded-faced rabbi dared, with a straight face, to speak to demons, forgive sinners, command summer squalls to settle down and cadavers to stand up.

Does it not at times seem absurd? A bit of a stretch? A reach?

The teachings of Christ don't give me pause. The thought of a Middle Eastern rabbi speaking wise words about loving neighbors and guarding the tongue is perfectly within reason.

But to say that this teacher had (and has) the authority to forgive sins, that he had (and has) the purity to serve as a sacrifice for sins, and that he had (and has) the audacity to receive worship—not just appreciation and admiration—but worship?

Come on now. Where does it stop? It sure didn't stop with his crucifixion. The hinge on the door called Gospel is a story about a dead man who stopped being dead, a buried man who unburied himself, a human heart that went stone-statue still for well more than three days and then, as sure as the sun shines at dawn, began pumping blood as it had ever since its first heartbeat in Mary's womb. The corpse woke up. Christ stood up. And billions, yes billions, of us have dared to believe that he is standing up for us still today. And that he is coming for us someday. That he will once and for all make sense of this mess we call humanity.

Be honest now. Does it not on occasion sound a bit far-fetched?

For some of you the answer is no. Your faith is sequoia strong, deep rooted, and shade giving.

Others of us, however, have to work through it. We have legitimate questions concerning Christianity. We seek answers that will satisfy our quest for an honest faith. If this describes you, let me welcome you to the Society of Seekers. Let me assure you, it is permissible to have doubts. Questions are steps upon which we ascend in the direction of heaven. The ascent can be steep, but the difficulty is no indication that we aren't making progress.

John made the ascent. His miracle stories are a form of handrails to aid us. Remember the reason he recorded them? "These are written that you may believe that Jesus is the Messiah, the

Son of God, and that by believing you may have life in his name" (John 20:31 NIV). John did not collect these stories so we might be informed or entertained. He wanted us to believe that Jesus is the Messiah. For that reason, for the benefit of us who question, he carefully described the pivotal moment in his life: the moment he first believed.

Speaking of himself, John wrote, "he saw and believed" (John 20:8). That phrase does not follow the water-to-wine miracle. John had no such reaction to the storm-walking Jesus or crowd-feeding Jesus. John was a follower when Jesus healed the blind man. But when did John become a believer? I'll let him tell you.

> Later, Joseph from Arimathea asked Pilate if he could take the body of Jesus. (Joseph was a secret follower of Jesus, because he was afraid of some of the leaders.) Pilate gave his permission, so Joseph came and took Jesus' body away. Nicodemus, who earlier had come to Jesus at night, went with Joseph. He brought about seventy-five pounds of myrrh and aloes. These two men took Jesus' body and wrapped it with the spices in pieces of linen cloth, which is how they bury the dead. In the place where Jesus was crucified, there was a garden. In the garden was a new tomb that had never been used before. (John 19:38–41 NCV)

As the sun set on Friday, the Son of God was set in a Jerusalem tomb. Two disciples prepared the body of Jesus for burial: Joseph of Arimathea and Nicodemus. Both men were affluent. Both were city leaders. Both were stealth followers who went public with their faith in the final days.

They had nothing to gain in this act of service. As far as they knew, they would be the final people to see their Savior. They prepared a dead body for burial, not a soon-to-be-risen body for a miracle.

They doused linen strips in a hundred pounds of burial spices (John 19:39),[1] which was a significant amount, "enough spices for the burial of a king."[2] Then they swaddled the corpse until it was tightly secure. Much in the same way we would wrap an elastic bandage around an injured ankle, they wrapped the entire body. The spices were intended to defer the smell of decomposition and, in time, to harden the wrap into a protective cover. They then looped a strip of linen beneath his chin and over the crown of his head to keep the mouth from falling open.[3] Upon completion of their work, the two men carried the body to the graveyard and placed it in an unused tomb.

From within a virgin womb Jesus was born. In a virgin tomb he was buried. At the insistence of the religious leaders, Pilate stationed guards at the tomb. They were told to keep the disciples out. No one mentioned the need of keeping Jesus in.

Early on Sunday morning, while it was still dark, Mary Magdalene came to the tomb and found that the stone had been rolled away from the entrance. (John 20:1 NLT)

It had been three days since the crucifixion. Jesus had promised that on the third day he would rise (Mark 8:31; 9:31; 10:34).

Friday was day one. Saturday was day two.

Friday evening was quiet. Saturday was sad.

On Friday the devils danced. On Saturday the demons feasted.

On Friday the disciples fled. On Saturday they wept.

On Friday heaven's finest Son died and was buried. On Saturday he spoke not a word.

On Friday the angels lowered their heads. On Saturday they kept their vigil.

But on Sunday, on the third day, in the predawn hours, in the heart of Joseph's tomb, the heart of Jesus began to beat.

Oh, to have seen the moment. To have heard the sudden intake of air. To have observed the eyes of Jesus blink open and seen a smile. Don't you know a smile spread across the Victor's face! The first breath of Christ meant the final breath of death.

What follows in John's gospel is a series of discoveries and celebrations. Mary Magdalene saw the empty tomb and assumed the worst. She hurried to awaken Peter and John with the news: "They have taken away the Lord out of the tomb, and we do not know where they have laid Him" (John 20:2).

John and Peter raced to the cemetery. John was faster, but Peter was bolder. He entered the tomb and came out bewildered. John entered the tomb and came out believing. "Then the other disciple, who came to the tomb first, went in also; and he saw and believed" (v. 8).

I have to think that John paused after he wrote that last word. *Believed. Believe* was his favorite verb. He used it eighty-eight times in his gospel! Twice as often as Matthew, Mark, and Luke combined.[4] *Believe* means more than mere credence. It signifies reliance upon and confidence in.

I experienced the dynamic of belief sometime back. I was spending a Saturday with some guys at a friend's cabin at the nearby Guadalupe River. The fall weather was warm, and the river water was high. We took advantage of a blue-skied afternoon to explore the riverside. We came upon an elegant, stately oak tree with a thick branch that stretched halfway across the water. An old rope hung from the end of the branch, dangling dead center over the river.

You can imagine our thoughts. *Yes, it's November. The water is cold. We are middle aged and blue jeaned, . . . but wouldn't a splash be fun?*

Using a long stick, we retrieved the rope. Though weathered and frayed, it *seemed* strong. Though the tree was old, the branch *looked* sturdy. But would it hold us? Or would it snap at the first tug, dumping a would-be swimmer in the shallow mud?

Sometime in the midst of rope testing and water dabbling, one fellow was filled with certain courage. "I'm going in!" He grabbed the rope and ran at the river as if it were a football field goal line. He leaped and flew. We gulped and watched. The branch bent and the rope stretched. But it held him, and he held on until he flew halfway to Dallas. He splashed and surfaced, and we didn't need an invitation to follow suit.

At what point did we believe in the strength of the rope? When we retrieved it? When we examined it? No, we believed when we placed our weight on it.

This is what John did. He cast his weight on Christ.

"He saw and believed."

What prompted his decision? John had yet to see the face of Jesus, hear the voice of Jesus, or touch the body of Jesus. All of that would come later. But as of this moment none of those things had happened. Yet John believed. What evidence, then, led to his confession?

Here is what he tells us: along with Peter "he . . . saw the strips of linen cloth lying there" (John 20:5 NCV). John used a Greek term for *lying* that means "still in their folds"[5] or in their "original convolutions."[6] "The body is missing but the clothes appear undisturbed."[7] The perfumed linen wrap was exactly the way Joseph and Nicodemus had left it on Friday evening, with one glaring exception. Jesus was not in it. He had fled the cocoon.[8]

John stared at the vacated shell and processed the evidence.

First there was the empty tomb. Grave robbers did not steal the body of Jesus. They would not have painstakingly extracted it from the burial wrap. Why would they? They had no motive and likely no time to do so.

Friends of Christ did not take the body. Why add indignity to death by removing Christ from the burial shroud? If for some reason they wanted to, the still-intact wrap said they didn't.

Then there was the matter of the linen head cloth. "He also saw the cloth that had been around Jesus' head, which was folded up and laid in a different place from the strips of linen" (v. 7 NCV). Again, grave robbers had no motive to remove the wrappings. If they had, they would have tossed the wrappings in the corner. The same for the friends of Jesus. Why remove the linen, double it over, and set it to the side?

John did the math: the stone rolled away, the now-tenantless tomb, the linens in their original state. Only one explanation made sense. Jesus himself did this! He passed through the burial wrap as if it were a sunrise mist.

John saw the cloth and believed. He trusted in Christ in the way we trusted in the rope. What a moment it must have been for him.

Maybe he ran his hand along the vacant slab or spotted prints of pierced feet on the dusty floor. No doubt he inhaled the sweet fragrance of a hundred pounds of spices that still hung in the air. What was intended to honor the dead now served to christen a King.

Perhaps John elbowed his friend who stood next to him in the empty tomb. "He's alive, Pete! No one took him. No one could kill him. He rolled away the rock so we could come in. Come on, I'll race you! First one back gets to write the gospel!"

John saw and believed.

I recall the moment in my life when I saw and believed. I began following Christ at the age of twenty, but somewhere around the age of twenty-two or twenty-three, I began to have some doubts. I admitted to a friend, "I'm not sure I really believe." His reply was simply, "Then, Max, here is the question. Where is the body of the crucified Christ?"

I've come to learn that his logic was Christian Apologetics 101. The line of reasoning goes like this: If Jesus didn't step out of the tomb, if his body is still in the grave . . .

Why didn't his enemies produce it? They knew where the body was buried. One display of the corpse and the church would have died in the cradle.

Why didn't the public deny it? On the day of pentecost, a brief fifty days after the resurrection, preaching to more than three thousand people in Jerusalem, the apostle Peter "spoke of the resurrection of the Messiah, that he was not abandoned to the realm of the dead, nor did his body see decay. God has raised this Jesus to life, and we are all witnesses of it" (Acts 2:31–32 NIV).

In my imagination I hear the apostles who were in the Upper Room shout, "Amen," the hundred and twenty followers who received the Holy Spirit on pentecost declare, "Amen," and the more than five hundred followers who witnessed the resurrected Lord (1 Cor. 15:6) agree, "Amen." No one—apparently no one— could say otherwise.

Don't you know they would have if they could have? The enemies of Christ would have gladly silenced Peter's sermon. But they had nothing to say. They had no body to display. Their silence, as it turns out, was the most convincing sermon of all.

The resurrection of Christ is the cornerstone of the Christian gospel. Paul, the apostle, was blunt: "If Christ has not been raised, your faith is worthless and powerless" (1 Cor. 15:17 AMP). If he has been raised, we could counter, then our faith is precious and powerful.

Accept the Easter invitation. Enter the tomb. Examine the facts. Even more, consider the implications. Because of the resurrection, a clearheaded, reasoned-out faith is a possibility.

Jesus welcomes an honest examination of the resurrection claim. He knows it all sounds far-fetched. Faith is not our native language. Hesitant? Welcome. Cautious? Welcome. A lobotomy is not a prerequisite for Christianity. Jesus invites the Society of the Seekers to view his resurrected body.

Faith is not the absence of doubt. Faith is simply a willingness to keep asking the hard questions. As my mentor Lynn Anderson says, "Faith is the decision to follow the best light you have about God and not quit."

The stone is still rolled back. The head cloth is still folded. The wrapping is still vacant. Examine the evidence. Look and see if you, like John, believe.

CHAPTER 11

Breakfast with Jesus

*L*eonardo da Vinci's *The Last Supper* began to deteriorate almost as soon as it was finished. The causes were multiple. The artist was partly to blame. The Duke of Milan commissioned the wall painting around 1494 as part of the renovation of a convent. However, Da Vinci did not paint in fresco, so the pigment didn't adhere properly to the surface, and within twenty years the paint began flaking.

Then there was the environment. The refectory sits in a low-lying section of the city, prone to humidity, and the north wall Leonardo painted was damp.

The painting hasn't always received the best of care. For decades the painting was unprotected from the steam of a nearby kitchen and the candle smoke of the sanctuary. At one point a door was cut into the wall, slicing off Christ's feet. Under Napoleon the refectory was turned into a horse stable, and soldiers spent idle time throwing bricks at the masterpiece. A flood once filled the rectory with two feet of water for fifteen straight days, leaving the painting carpeted with green mold. On August 16, 1943, a Royal Air Force bomb hit the convent, destroying the roof of the refectory and a nearby cloister.

It's a wonder the painting still exists. That it does is a tribute to art restorationists. On numerous occasions experts have applied their skills to *The Last Supper*. They've been tireless in their devotion. The most recent effort at conservation lasted twenty-two years, from 1977 to 1999.[1]

Part historian, part chemist, the restorer asks one question: What was the original intent of the artist? Tools can include a pair of magnifying visors, a liter of acetone, brushes, cotton swabs, and synthetic varnish. Inch by exacting inch, art restorers mimic the brushstroke of the originator, reclaiming color and revealing genius.

Thanks to restorationists the work of Da Vinci can be admired.

Thanks to Jesus the work of his servants can be restored. The years take their toll on the purest of saints. Our souls get soiled. Our luster diminishes. We need cleaning up as well.

Proof is in the pages of Scripture. We call Abraham our hero, but he once refused to call his wife his wife. We delight in the words of David. Yet David was known to delight in the wife of a friend. Rahab is one of a handful of females in the genealogy of Jesus. She was also a madam in the world's oldest profession. Paul killed Christians before he taught them. James and John were "Sons of Thunder" before they were apostles of peace. The followers of Jesus squabbled like kids before they died like martyrs. The Bible is full of famous failures.

We name our children after them. We sing songs about them. We set out to imitate them. But let's be honest. There isn't a human in the Bible who didn't behave like one. They wore the pig slop of the prodigal, each and every one of them.

And so do we.

We'd be wise to admit it, to come clean and come out of hiding. We, too, have fallen flat, fallen hard, and fallen enough to leave us wondering how in God's name God names us as his own. I'm not talking about minor slipups, misdemeanors, and innocent mistakes. I'm calling to the surface the Jonah moments in which we turned from God, Elijah moments in which we ran from God, Jacob moments in which we dared to make a demand of God.

When you reflect on your darkest deeds, where do your memories take you? To a college campus? To an off-the-beaten-path motel? To a shady business transaction? What season of your life surfaces? Teenage rebellion for some. Middle-age crisis for others. Your days in the military? Your months on the foreign assignment? Did you abandon your friends? Abandon your post? Abandon your convictions?

Have you questioned whether God could ever use you again? If so, you need to turn to a story in the book of John: the miracle of Peter's restoration.

Restoration is the second stanza in the "Anthem of the Second Chance." In verse one God forgives us. In verse two God continually restores us to our place of service. He washes us, for sure. But he washes us for a reason—that we might once again be portraits of his goodness and hang in his gallery.

Did Jesus not do this with Peter?

Jesus' relationship with the apostle began on the Sea of Galilee three years prior to the crucifixion. Peter, a fisherman, had fished all night with his friends. Jesus, a carpenter, had preached on the shore all morning. The fishermen were fishless and clueless. Jesus told them where to toss their nets. Peter and the others could have, understandably, dismissed the instruction. They were tired. They wanted to rest. Besides, Jesus was a woodworker, not a net-caster. Still, to Peter's credit, he took the suggestion and nearly pulled a hamstring while dragging in the catch (Luke 5:1–7).

And so began this Rocky Mountain friendship between Jesus and Peter. "Rocky Mountain" because it was given to great peaks and pits, highs and lows. But no moment was lower than the night Peter broke his promise to Jesus.

It was the eve of the crucifixion. Christ had told his followers that they would all abandon him.

> Then Peter said to him, "Even if everyone should lose faith, I never will."
>
> "Believe me, Peter," returned Jesus, "this very night before the cock crows twice, you will disown me three times."
>
> But Peter protested violently, "Even if it means dying with you, I will never disown you!" And they all made the same protest. (Mark 14:29–31 PHILLIPS)

Peter's resolve was short lived. When the Romans arrested Jesus, Peter and the other followers ran like scalded dogs. Peter garnered enough courage to return to the mock trial. But not enough courage to enter the court. "Peter followed Him [Jesus] at a distance, right into the courtyard of the high priest. And he sat with the servants and warmed himself at the fire" (v. 54).

Thanks to the fire, his body grew warm. Thanks to his fear, his heart grew cold. When confronted about his association with Jesus, Peter denied he ever knew the man.

Peter swore, "A curse on me if I'm lying—I don't know this man you're talking about!" And immediately the rooster crowed the second time.

Suddenly, Jesus' words flashed through Peter's mind: "Before the rooster crows twice, you will deny three times that you even know me." And he broke down and wept. (vv. 71–72 NLT)

One gets the feeling that from this day forward the sound of a crowing rooster caused Peter to feel a knot in the pit of his stomach.

Christ went to the cross and died. Peter went into the shadows and hid. Friday was tragic. Saturday was silent. But Sunday? Christ placed his heel squarely on the head of Satan, the serpent of death, stood up, and walked out of the tomb. When the female followers saw the empty grave, the angel told them:

Don't be alarmed. . . . You are looking for Jesus the Nazarene, who was crucified. He has been resurrected! He is not here! See the place where they put Him. But go, tell His disciples and Peter, "He is going ahead of you to Galilee; you will see Him there just as He told you." (Mark 16:6–7 HCSB)

My goodness, did you see what I just saw? Peter had cursed the very name of Jesus. And yet the angel, no doubt on the instruction of Christ, told the women, "Make sure Peter gets the message. Don't let him miss out. Don't let him exclude himself. Don't let him think for a moment he is disqualified." It's as if all of heaven had watched Peter fall. Now all of heaven wanted to help him back on his feet.

When I was six years of age, my brother and I were playing a game of tag, running up and down the aisles of a grocery store. Mom told us to behave, but we did not listen. I recall turning a corner and looking up just in time to see a stand-alone display of honey. I crashed into it without tapping my brakes. Bottles flew every direction—glass bottles of honey! Shoppers stopped and stared. The store manager appeared.

"Whose boy are you?" he barked.

There I sat on the floor, covered with sticky. I looked at the honey. I looked at the manager. I wondered how many years in prison I was going to get. Then, from behind me, I heard the voice of my mom. "He belongs to me," she said. "We'll clean up this mess."

Jesus felt the same way about Peter: "He belongs to me. I can clean up this mess."

The cleanup would take place on the shore of the Sea of Galilee. Peter and the other followers traveled the eighty miles north to the sea. For reasons we are not told, they went fishing again. And "that night they caught nothing" (John 21:3). Again no fish. How is it that professional fishermen, raised on this very body of water, could spend all night on the sea and catch nary a minnow? And how is it that the stranger on the shoreline knew more than they about finding fish?

> But when the morning had now come, Jesus stood on the shore; yet the disciples did not know that it was Jesus. Then Jesus said to them, "Children, have you any food?"
>
> They answered Him, "No."
>
> And He said to them, "Cast the net on the right side of the boat, and you will find some." (vv. 4–6)

Is there a word in Aramaic for déjà vu? Surely the disciples remembered another night of fruitless toil on this very sea. The endless tossing of the net. Its slapping on the water. How the dusk became night. The stars came out, and the fish stayed deep. Finally the sun rose.

On that morning, like this one, a nonfisherman told them to try one more time. They did. What happened then, happened again. The net filled with flipping, flopping silver gills. They were suddenly fish flush, all because of a tip from an outsider. "They were not able to draw it in because of the multitude of fish" (v. 6).

That's all John needed. The stranger on the beach was a stranger to him no longer. "Therefore that disciple whom Jesus loved said to Peter, 'It is the Lord!' Now when Simon Peter heard that it was the Lord, he put on his outer garment (for he had removed it), and plunged into the sea" (v. 7).

Peter dove like a missile into the water. He swam to shore and climbed up on the beach, and when he walked toward Jesus, guess what he saw? "A fire of coals" (v. 9).

The last time a fire of coals was mentioned in the gospels, Peter was standing next to it, cussing like a sailor, denying the very name of Christ.

I think this fire of coals was Jesus' way of saying, "I know what you did. We need to talk." We might expect Jesus to go nuclear on Peter: dredge up the past, rehearse the promises Peter broke, call down every "I told you so" from heaven. He could have used his pierced hand to extend an accusing finger. "Did you learn your lesson, Peter?" A divine snarl or two seems in order.

But no. Just this: "Come and eat breakfast" (v. 12).

Jesus had coffee in the kettle.

Who would've imagined this invitation? Christ, just days earlier, died as a sin offering for humanity. He poleaxed the devil and turned every grave into short-term housing. Holding confetti and lining up for a Pearly Gate victory parade, heaven's angels were ready to celebrate. But the party would have to wait.

Jesus wanted to cook fish tacos for his friends. He wanted to restore the heart and the ministry of Peter. He perceived the layers of guilt and shame on the heart of his friend. As if with a cotton swab of grace, he began to wipe them away.

So when they had eaten breakfast, Jesus said to Simon Peter, "Simon, son of Jonah, do you love Me more than these?" (v. 15).

In my imagination Jesus gestured to the other disciples as he asked the question. Peter had said he did. "Everyone else may stumble in their faith because of you, but I will not" (Matt. 26:33 NCV). But Peter did fall, publicly and painfully. So Jesus restored him publicly and personally. Peter denied the Lord three times. The Lord, in response, asked three questions:

"Do you love Me more than these?" (John 21:15).

"Do you love Me?" (v. 16).

"Do you love Me?" (v. 17).

Peter seized the opportunity to repent of each denial with a confession.

"I love You" (v. 15).

"I love You" (v. 16).

"I love You" (v. 17).

Jesus used a strong word for love: *agape.* Peter replied with a more modest word for love that means "affection." His boasting was gone. His heart was honest. So Christ restored Peter with three personal commissions:

"Feed My lambs" (v. 15).

"Tend My sheep" (v. 16).

"Feed My sheep" (v. 17).

Jesus had work for Peter to do, flocks for Peter to pastor. The apostle was discouraged but not disqualified.

And you? Are you somewhere between the two fires? Have your fumbles and stumbles left you questioning your place in God's plan? If so, let this story remind you that Christ is not finished with you either. You might be down, but you are not out. You might feel alone, but you are not alone. Jesus went on a search and rescue mission for Peter. He will do the same for you. Jesus "can keep you on your feet" (Jude v. 24 THE MESSAGE).

Could you use some breakfast?

Jesus is the hero here. He is the one who found Peter, called Peter, orchestrated the fish catch for Peter, built the fire for Peter, cooked breakfast for Peter, took the confession of Peter, and recommissioned Peter. If the distance between Christ and Peter consisted of a hundred steps, Jesus took ninety-nine and a half.

But Peter still had to take his step.

He was told to meet Jesus in Galilee, so he went.

He heard Jesus was on the shore, so he jumped.

He was asked questions by Christ, so he answered.

He obeyed. He responded. He interacted. In other words he stayed in communion with Christ.

You'll want to do anything but that. Failure sires denial. And denial wants to avoid the very One we need. Don't give in to the desire. Head in the direction of Jesus. Speak to Jesus, and listen as he speaks to you. Obey him.

For some of you restoration is the miracle you need. You

admire the story of the blind man seeing or the crippled man walking. You're inspired by the abundance of bread and the overflowing vats of wine. But what you need is restoration.

Jesus wants to give it to you.

He has certainly restored me. More times than I can count I've seen Jesus standing on the shoreline. On one of those occasions he sure looked a lot like my wife. The story began with the purchase of a new smartphone. I'd upgraded from a flip phone to one that allowed me to access the Internet. I've always been cautious about the Internet. It unnerves me to think that I am at any point a click or two away from seeing images of women that I have no right to see. For that reason I've placed filters on everything I own.

But when it came to my first smartphone, well, I wasn't smart. I took it into my office, unpacked it, and plugged it in. *Wow, I can access the news, the sports, my e-mails, all right here from my phone*, I realized. Then the thought hit me. *Is this device protected?*

Here is what I should have done: walk down the hall and hand the phone to our tech team. Yet here is what I did: I entered some words that would allow an unprotected device to access an immoral world. In a matter of seconds she appeared on the screen. I did not look long, but any amount of time is too long.

I turned off the phone, put it in my pocket, and leaned back in my chair. *What did you just do?* I asked myself. I resolved to have a filter placed on it. But when I called, our tech team had left the building for the day. So I drove home.

Even though it's been nearly a decade since that evening, I recall it vividly. Denalyn was cooking. I walked into the kitchen and emptied my pockets on the cabinet. She spotted my new phone and picked it up.

"Oh, a new phone?" She opened the screen, and to my horror the picture was still there.

The hurt on her face broke my heart. My explanation felt slippery and shallow. A tense cloud settled over the evening. We tried to talk, but the emotion was raw. I hardly slept. When I climbed out of bed, the sky was still dark. So was my soul.

I stepped into the bathroom and flipped on the light. That is when I realized Denalyn was already awake. She was not in the bathroom, but she had been. On my mirror was a three-foot-tall lipstick heart that she had drawn. In the middle of it she wrote the words "I forgive you. I love you."

Peter received breakfast on the beach. Max got lipstick on the mirror. We both received grace. Pure grace.

No one makes it through life failure-free. No one. Peter didn't. Jacob didn't. King David didn't. Solomon didn't. I haven't, and you won't. There is within each of us the capacity to do the very thing we resolve to avoid. At some point the stallions within break down the corral, and we—for a moment, a day, or a decade—run wild.

If this has happened to you, remember the seaside breakfast.

When this happens to you, remember the seaside breakfast.

Jesus still gives what he gave Peter: complete and total restoration.

Peter went on to preach the inaugural sermon of the church. On the day of pentecost, he was privileged to present the initial proclamation of the gospel. As we envision him standing before the Jerusalem crowd, let's remember that less than two months earlier he was standing before the charcoal fire. Can anyone turn a denying Peter into a proclaiming Peter? Jesus can.

He did then.

He does still.

CHAPTER 12

Believe, Just Believe

*P*erhaps you can envision a middle-aged man going goofy in the motel swimming pool. His four-year-old daughter stands on the edge and watches. Her mom sits on a pool chair and sighs. Other guests cast a glance at the man and wonder about his sanity. That is, unless they've ever done what he is doing. If so, they empathize.

It's not easy convincing a kid to jump into the pool. It was time, I believed, for Jenna to take the plunge. She wasn't so sure. She stood on the pool's edge, toes gripping the concrete, arms clutching herself, eyes watching her dad—yours truly—perform every aquatic, acrobatic, underwater, synchronized swimming trick I knew.

"See, it's fun!" I'd say and float on my back or drop to the bottom or pretend I was a beluga whale and swim to the other side.

I really wanted Jenna to jump, to swim, to enter the wonderful world of water. I grew up a bike ride away from a public pool where twenty-five cents would get you a summer's day full of high dives, belly flops, and enough Marco Polo games to turn fingers into fins.

"I'll catch you!" I told Jenna. "You'll love it!" I told Jenna. "Just trust me!" I told Jenna. And finally she did.

She jumped. She took the plunge. She made the step. She moved from the "edge of the pool" to "into the pool."

I caught her, as I promised.

She survived, as I promised she would.

And she loved it. All because she believed.

We preachers tend to complicate this thing of belief. We get technical, seek precision. We've been known to write papers about the exact moment of salvation and the evidence of repentance. We've hashed and rehashed what needs to be known and what needs to be done.

Call me simple, but I think God is a good Father. I think he knows something about life. And I think he invites us to take the step, to take the plunge, to jump—not into a pool but into a relationship with him that is vibrant, joyous, and, yes, fun! It's not always easy, mind you. But certainly it's worth the risk, and by all means it's better than life in a deck chair on the poolside.

I've no reason to think John knew anything about convincing a child to swim. But I'd like to think he'd approve of my illustration on faith. His gospel could well have been subtitled *That You May Believe.*

Why tell about the water-to-wine miracle? So you would believe that Jesus can restore what life has taken.

Why tell us about the faith of a nobleman? That you might believe Jesus hears your prayers though you think he doesn't.

Why tell about the lame man who took up his mat or the blind man who washed the mud from his eyes? That you might believe in a Jesus who sees a new version of us and gives new vision to us.

Why walk on water, feed the thousands, and raise the dead? That you would believe God still stills the storms of life, still solves the problems of life, and still brings the dead to life.

Need grace? Jesus' work of redemption is still finished.

Need reassurance that it's all true? The tomb is still empty.

Need a second chance? The coal fire is still burning on the Galilean shore.

All these events stand together as one voice, cheering you on, calling on you to believe that this miracle-working God cares for you, fights for you, and will come to your aid.

These miracles are in your life what the basketball players and fans were to Luke, a young player whose dream came true in the final game of the year.

Luke learns at a different pace than the other elementary school kids. He develops more slowly than his peers. Yet he has a winsome smile and a pure heart that endears him to everyone who knows him.

When the pastor of the church formed a basketball team, Luke signed up. While the other boys practiced dribbling and layups, Luke threw the ball at the basket from the free throw line. It rarely went in, but when it did, Luke raised his arms and shouted, "Look at me, Coach! Look at me!" The coach looked at him. And smiled.

The team didn't fare too well that season. They won only once. And that victory was the consequence of a snowstorm that kept the other team from showing up. In the final game of the year, they played the best team in the league. It was over as soon as it began. Near the end of the last quarter, Luke's team stood nearly thirty points behind. It was then that one of the boys called time-out. "Coach," he said, "this is our last game, and Luke has never made a basket. I think we should let him into the game."

The team agreed. The coach placed him near the free throw line and instructed him to wait.

Luke was ecstatic. He stood on his spot. When the ball was passed to him, he shot and missed. A player for the other team snatched the rebound and dribbled down the court for an easy basket. Luke was handed the ball again. He shot and missed again. The other team scored off the rebound.

Gradually the other team began to figure out what was going on. When they did, they got in on the action. They began throwing the ball to Luke. He kept missing, so the players from both teams kept throwing it to him. Soon everyone in the gym was pulling for Luke to make a basket.

The coach was sure that time must have expired. The game had to be over. He glanced at the official clock. It was stopped at 4.3 seconds. Turns out even the timekeepers were in on the effort. They stood by their table, shouting with the crowd, "Luke! Luke!"

Luke shot and shot. He attempted again and again and again and finally, miraculously, one of his shots took a crazy bounce on the rim. Everyone held their breath. The ball dropped in. The place erupted! Luke's arms sprang up in the air, and he shouted, "I won! I won!" His team escorted him off the court, the clock ticked down, and the game was over.[1]

I see some gospel in that story. I see a picture of God's devotion to you and me. God wants us to win. Not win in basketball necessarily, but win in faith, in hope, in life. He wants us to win for eternity. He marshals every force, enlists every tool, employs every miracle so you and I will someday throw triumphant fists into the sky.

Can I urge you to see the miracles of Jesus as part of his arsenal? They were, and are, part of the collective chant from heaven, crying your name and mine, calling upon us to believe.

He still sends this invitation through miracles.

A dear member of our congregation has battled a curved spine for the entirety of her young life. It has impeded her growth and sleep. Then when she was twenty, doctors discovered a rapidly growing tumor in the same area. She went in for surgery but not before she sought the prayer support of many of us.

She awoke from the surgery to hear the amazed physician say, "What I saw on the X-ray and saw in the operating room were two different things. Your spine is healthy. There is no tumor. I have no explanation."[2]

Coincidence? Or a sign from God to remind her of his presence?

For more than twenty years Mark Bouman directed a Christian orphanage in Cambodia. He and his wife ran every detail of the mission, from drilling water wells to caring for sick children. The orphans called Mark their Papa, and he regarded them as his children. That is why his heart broke when he and his family had to flee Cambodia suddenly in 1975 due to an insurrection. He was able to travel safely to Thailand but couldn't quit thinking about the children. After two weeks he received an impassioned call from an orphanage worker, begging him to return and help them.

He hurried to the airport in Bangkok. It was in a state of chaos. Dozens of people were trying to buy a ticket on a flight to

Cambodia. The ticket agent was shouting over the crowd, "We have no more tickets!" Mark didn't know what to do.

He then noticed another airline counter. No one stood in line at their desk. He walked over and asked the ticket agent if there was a seat available for Cambodia. "Yes," she said, "there is a seat available. May I have your passport?"

Within two hours Mark was landing in Cambodia.[3]

An airline with no person in line? One ticket available?

Coincidence? Or God-incident?

Yesterday morning I placed a call to a credit card customer service department. I had an issue with mine. The issue was not a pressing one as evidenced by the fact that I'd been intending to make the call for two months. The item kept getting bumped off the priority section of my to-do list. Once I made the call, however, I suspected that something else, or Someone, had caused the delay.

When I told the representative my name, she said, "Max Lucado? *The* Max Lucado?"

Two types of people respond to my name this way: my parole officers and readers of my books. I hoped she was part of the latter.

She was. She began telling me how my books have kept her encouraged over the years, how she keeps one at her bedside, and . . . About that moment she got choked up. Seriously choked up. She couldn't talk. For the better part of a minute, neither one of us said anything. She wept quietly.

She then gathered herself and apologized for not behaving in a professional manner. Her tears didn't bother me, I told her. And I asked what was going on.

She explained that she had just returned from a doctor's visit where she had been told that she suffers from congestive heart failure. The news devastated her. En route to her office she called her husband. No answer. She called her son. No answer. She could barely contain her tears as she entered her office building. Needing to talk to someone, she prayed, *Lord, can you let me share my burden with someone? Anyone?*

She walked to her desk and sat down, and I was the next call she took.

What are the odds? Of all the customer service personnel, she was the one who took my call. Of all the days I could have called, that was the day I called.

On and on and on these stories could go.

Explain them away if you wish. Chalk them up to random events. Or allow them to achieve their intended purpose: to remind us that we are under the care of God's ever-present help. We are not weather vanes whipped about by the winds of fate and chance. We are the children of a mighty and good God who cares for us.

John's hope was that we would believe, that unbelievers would begin believing and believers would keep believing that "Jesus is the Christ, the Son of God" (John 20:31).

There it is. The hope of John, the hope of his book, indeed the hope of God, and the hope of *this* book. That we would believe, not in our power, not in humanity's ability to help itself, not in tarot cards or good fortune, not in good looks or good luck. But that we would believe in Jesus. Jesus as the Christ, the Messiah, the Anointed One. Jesus as the Son of God.

The message of the miracles is the Miracle Worker himself. He wants you to know you are never alone. You are never without help, hope, or strength. You are stronger than you think because God is nearer than you might imagine.

He wants you to know:

I know everything about you (Ps. 139:1).

I know when you sit down and when you rise up (Ps. 139:2).

I've numbered the hairs on your head (Matt. 10:29–31).

I've adopted you into my family (Rom. 8:15).

Before you were the size of a freckle in your mother's womb, I knew you (Jer. 1:4–5).

You are my idea, and I have only good ideas (Eph. 1:11–12).

You won't live a day longer or less than I intend (Ps. 139:16).

I love you as my own child (1 John 3:1).

I will take care of you (Matt. 6:31–33).

None of this love 'em and leave 'em stuff with me. I love you with an everlasting love (Jer. 31:3).

I can't quit thinking about you (Ps. 139:17–18).

You are my treasured possession (Ex. 19:5).

Let's do great things together (Jer. 33:3).

Nothing will ever separate you from my love (Rom. 8:38–39).

I began this final chapter with a father story. Might I conclude with one more?

When my daughters were small, I made a practice of returning from travel with a gift for each one. I would walk through the door and yell, "Daddy's home!" and they would scurry to give me a hug. It did not bother me when they would ask, "What did you bring us?" I wasn't insulted when they would take the new toy and scamper off to play. In part I needed to rest. Even more, I knew they would come back. At some point before bedtime, freshly bathed and wearing pajamas, they'd climb up on my lap. We'd read a book or I'd tell a story, and soon they'd fall asleep.

I knew it wasn't my presents that brought them comfort. It was my presence.

May God bless your life with more miracles than you can count. May your water become cabernet. May your dark storms turn into springtime sun. May he feed thousands upon thousands through your picnic basket of faith. May you walk like the just-healed cripple, see like the was-blind man, live like the was-dead Lazarus. May you dwell in the grace of the cross, the hope of the empty tomb, and the assurance of restoration power. But most of all may you believe—believe that God is your ever-present help. And in his presence may you find rest.

Questions for Reflection

PREPARED BY ANDREA LUCADO

CHAPTER 1

We Can't, but God Can

1. What do you think about miracles?
   - Do you believe the Bible's miracle stories?
   - Why or why not?
   - Do you believe that miracles occur in this present day?
   - Have you witnessed or experienced a miracle? If so, tell the story.
   - If not, do you know someone who claims to have witnessed or experienced a miracle? What were those circumstances?

2. Of the miracles recorded in Scripture, which is your favorite?
   - What about this miracle intrigues you?
   - What does this miracle say about Jesus' heart for others?

3. What does Max say is unique about John's gospel?

   If you had been a disciple of Jesus and were recording your own gospel about his life, what would have been your focus, and why?

4. John 20:30–31 says, "Jesus performed many other signs in the presence of his disciples, which are not recorded in this book. But these are written that you may believe that Jesus is the Messiah, the Son of God, and that by believing you may have life in his name" (NIV).
   • Spend a moment imagining miracles that weren't recorded in Scripture. Imagine the people healed, forgiven, saved. Who are you in that scene?
   • According to Max what does "life in his name" look like? (See p. 4.)

5. What else do the miracles of Christ promise us? (See p. 5.) How does this affect your faith?

6. The woman Max describes at the beginning of this chapter said, "It's just me, and I ain't much."
   • Have you ever felt like this? If so, what circumstances caused you to feel this way?
   • Is there any area of your life right now in which you feel alone? Describe the situation or events that led up to this. How has this loneliness affected you?
   • How has loneliness affected your faith?
   • What words would you use to describe this lonely season?

7. Max cites a study from Parkland Hospital in Dallas. What did that study discover?
   • How did you react to this information? Did it surprise you? Why or why not?
   • Have you witnessed loneliness in your family or on a

large communal scale in your city or neighborhood? Give some examples.

- The hospital study revealed that these patients ultimately wanted to know that someone cared (p. 7). In what way can you relate to that sentiment?

8. Max asks, "Do you believe in a Jesus who has not only power but a passionate love for the weak and wounded of the world? Do you think he cares enough about you to find you in the lonely waiting rooms, rehab centers, and convalescent homes of life?" (p. 8).
   - How would you answer these questions?
   - What personal experiences have led you to this belief in the Jesus of power and love?

9. Fill in the blanks: "And we will be careful, oh so careful, to see the signs as John designed them to be seen, not as entries in a _____ ____, but as samples from God's _____" (p. 6).
   - Explain the statement above.
   - What do you hope to learn about Jesus in this book?
   - What do you hope to learn about miracles?
   - What do you hope to learn about yourself?

10. The gospel of Matthew ends with these words of Jesus: "And behold, I am with you always, to the end of the age" (Matt. 28:20 ESV).
    - Imagine you are John listening to Jesus telling you these words. How would you feel?
    - What does this promise mean to you today?

11. Revisit John 20:30–31.
    - Which phrase in these verses is most meaningful to you? Why?
    - When John promises that believing leads to "life in [Jesus'] name," what do you think he is trying to convey? What does "life in his name" mean to you?

CHAPTER 2

He Will Replenish What Life Has Taken

1. Read the story of Jesus' first miracle in John 2:1–12.

2. What do you think was the purpose of this miracle?

3. Imagine the scene.
   • What did the guests in this story lack?
   • What was Jesus' initial response to Mary in verse 4 when she told him they had no more wine?
   • Why did he respond this way?
   • Why do you think Mary considered the lack of wine a problem urgent enough to bring it to Jesus?

4. Initially Jesus was hesitant to perform this miracle, saying, "Dear woman, that's not our problem. . . . My time has not yet come" (John 2:4 NLT). What did Jesus mean by "My time has not yet come"? Mary responded by turning to the servants and instructing them, "Do whatever he tells you" (v. 5 NLT).
   • Why did Mary intervene?

• What do you think Mary knew about Jesus?

Regarding this passage Max says, "*Whatever* means whatever. Whatever he says, whatever he commands. Even if his 'whatever' is a *nothing whatsoever*, do it" (p. 20). Have you ever been hesitant to bring a need to Jesus because you were worried about what the "whatever" might mean for you? If so, describe what that need was or is.

5. Fill in the blank: "Be anxious for nothing, but in _____ by prayer and supplication, with thanksgiving, let your requests be made known to God" (Phil. 4:6). Based on this verse, what should we *not* bring to God in prayer?

6. What is something you lack right now? Time? Health? Funds? How does this lack affect your daily life, your relationships with others, and your faith? Have you brought this need to Christ? Why or why not?
   • If you have brought this need to Christ in prayer, what has been the response?
   • If you haven't, consider what might be preventing you from doing so. What holds you back?

7. Jesus eventually met the need of the wedding guests that night. What is Max's explanation for Jesus' decision to provide the miracle-produced wine? (See p. 17.)

8. What was the quality of the wine Jesus made? (See John 2:9–10.)
   • Jesus could have made less wine. He could have made a

poorer quality wine. As the master of ceremonies said, "A host always serves the best wine first. . . . Then, when everyone has had a lot to drink, he brings out the less expensive wine. But you have kept the best until now!" (John 2:10 NLT). Many probably didn't notice how good the wine was that night, so why did Jesus perform this miracle in the way he did?

- What does this story tell you about how Jesus will respond to your needs?

9. In his letter to the Ephesians, Paul wrote, "Now to Him who is able to do exceedingly abundantly above all that we ask or think, according to the power that works in us, to Him be glory in the church by Christ Jesus to all generations, forever and ever. Amen" (Eph. 3:20–21).

- Have you ever given more than was asked by a loved one? Perhaps you gave your grandchild two cookies instead of one, or you gave your son the cash he needed for gas *and* a soda, or you helped a friend move and then stayed around to hang curtains and get her settled.
- Why did you give in abundance? What prompted you to exceed the request? How did the gift make you feel?
- If you can give in abundance to those around you with the resources you have as a human, what do you think the God of the universe is capable of giving you when you bring your needs to him?

CHAPTER 3

The Long Walk Between Offered and Answered Prayer

1. Are you waiting for an answer to prayer? Explain your prayer, and consider what could be God's reasons for giving you a season of waiting.

2. Imagine you are on a road. The starting point is your offered prayer. The destination is that prayer answered. What part of the road are you on today? What has this journey been like for you?

3. Read John 4:46–47.
   - What was the distance from Capernaum to Cana? (See p. 27.)
   - Why do you think the official traveled that far to see Jesus?
   - What did the official do to Jesus in verse 47?
   - Have you ever begged God for something? What was it? Why did you feel desperate enough to beg?
   - If God didn't answer your prayer as you wanted, did it affect your faith? Why or why not?

4. How did Jesus respond to the official's plea in John 4:48?
   - What does Max give as a possible reason for Jesus' response? (See p. 28.)
   - How did the official respond to Jesus in John 4:49? Would you have responded this way? Why or why not?

5. John 4:50 says, "Then Jesus told him, 'Go back home. Your son will live!' And the man believed what Jesus said and started home" (NLT).
   - What emotions or thoughts would you have experienced on that eighteen-mile journey from Cana to your home in Capernaum?
   - What emotions or thoughts have you experienced on your current journey since your prayer was first offered?
   - What is the difference between your journey and the official's?

6. Based on your experience, how would you answer this question: "How do we walk by faith when we are thus far blind to the solution?" (p. 31).

7. Psalm 46:1 says, "God is our refuge and strength, an ever-present help in trouble" (NIV).
   - What kind of help does God provide us during trouble?
   - Describe a time you were aware of his being ever present. How did you experience his presence? How did it affect your strength or confidence or joy?
   - If you have not experienced the ever-present God, has a friend or loved one been by your side during a difficult

time? How did it strengthen you to have that person's presence in the midst of trouble?

8. Read the rest of the official's story in John 4:51–53.
   - In addition to healing the official's son, what did this miracle accomplish?
   - Have you ever seen a greater purpose for your journey from offered prayer to answered prayer?
   - Or has God ever revealed a different plan as you waited for him to answer your prayer? If so, how did you initially react to that plan? In hindsight do you see his purpose in that plan?

9. Jesus told the official, "Go back home. Your son will live!" (John 4:50 NLT). How did the official respond? How could you respond to Jesus in a similar way? Not knowing what's ahead on your journey of waiting, not knowing if God will answer your prayer as you wish, how could you believe what Jesus said in Scripture and continue your journey home?

CHAPTER 4

Stand Up, Take Up, and Walk

1. At the beginning of this chapter, Max suggests that we've all been stuck: "Mired in the mud of resentment, bogged down in debt, trapped in a dead-end career, up to your waist in the swamp of an unsolvable conflict. Stuck" (p. 38).
   • Is there an area of your life today where you feel stuck?
   • If so, in what way are you stuck, and how long have you felt this way?
   • Why are you stuck in this particular area of your life?

2. Matthew 9:35–36 says, ". . . wherever [Jesus] went he healed people of every sort of illness. And what pity he felt for the crowds that came, because their problems were so great and they didn't know what to do or where to go for help" (TLB).
   • Have you ever felt like the crowd described in this passage—that you were facing a problem so great you didn't know what to do or where to go? If so, describe what that was like for you and how it affected your feelings of being stuck.

- Is there an area of "stuckness" in your life today? Explain.
- Considering where you feel stuck in your life today, or perhaps when you felt stuck in the past, where could you go for help?

3. Read John 5:1–6.
   - How long had the lame man been an invalid?
   - How would you feel about your circumstances if you had been suffering from the same illness or plight for thirty-eight years?
   - What is the longest season of suffering or illness you have endured? What caused this period of suffering?
   - How has suffering affected your life, your emotions, and your faith?
   - What question did Jesus ask the lame man in verse 6?
   - How did the lame man respond?
   - If Jesus asked you the same question about a situation you have felt stuck in, how would you answer him?

4. Max poses Jesus' question a different way: "Are you ready to get unstuck?" (p. 41).
   - What are some reasons a person might want to remain stuck?
   - Have you ever remained stuck even though you knew there was a way out? Why did you choose to stay stuck?

5. What did Jesus tell the lame man in John 5:8?

6. Max breaks verse 8 into three actions to take when you feel stuck. What does Max say these actions mean?

    Stand up:

    Pick up your mat:

    Walk:

    • Considering an area where you feel stuck today, how could you . . .

      stand up?

      pick up your mat?

      walk?

    • Which of these three steps is most difficult for you, and why?

7. Max tells the story of Barbara Snyder, a talented gymnast who fell chronically ill and was miraculously healed. Max writes, "Christ performed the miracle. Christ intervened." But what did Barbara have to do? (See p. 43.)

8. Fill in the blank: "believe in the Jesus who believes in ___." Often our "stuckness" becomes our identity. We are afraid to move on because who are we without our problem, pain, or sickness? But as Max says, "[Jesus] believes that you can rise up, take up, and move on. You are stronger than you think." Do you believe this about yourself? Why or why not?

9. Like the widower that Max writes about at the end of this chapter, write down some of your "I can't"s on a piece of paper. Consider your list.

- How long have some of these "I can't"s been part of your life?
- How many of them do you have the power to change?
- How many of them are you afraid to change?
- Now bury your list or burn it or trash it. Do something that physically symbolizes you are not held back by your "I can't"s. You can surrender them to God.

CHAPTER 5

We Can Solve This

1. What small or mundane problem easily overwhelms or frustrates you? Traffic? Piles of dirty laundry? A full inbox?

   • How do you typically respond when you're facing this overwhelming scenario?

   • What is it about this situation that overwhelms you?

   • In the past what strategies have you used to counter an overwhelming situation?

   • Now think about a serious problem in your life that currently feels overwhelming.

2. In this chapter you read about the miracle of Jesus' feeding the five thousand. Max points out that while five thousand men had gathered that day, this didn't include the women and children, meaning the crowd could have been as large as fifteen thousand.

   • What's the biggest crowd you've fed? Or what's the biggest gathering you were part of in which people were fed?

   • List all the steps you can think of that would be required to plan for and to feed a large crowd.

- Now imagine you had to feed fifteen thousand people. What additional work, planning, and money would this require?

3. In John 6:5 Jesus asked Philip, "Where can we buy enough bread to feed all these people?" (Bruner translation).

   Philip responded, "Several thousand dollars' worth of bread wouldn't be enough to give even a tiny bite to all these people!" (v. 7 Bruner translation).

   Andrew responded, "There is a boy here with five loaves of barley bread and two fish. Oh, but what are these things when there are all these people?" (v. 9 Bruner translation).
   - Why do you think Philip responded the way he did?
   - Why do you think Andrew responded the way he did?
   - If Jesus knew what was going to happen, why do you think he asked this question?
   - What do the disciples' responses indicate about their understanding of Jesus' power?

4. Andrew and Philip faced different obstacles in trying to feed that large crowd in Galilee.
   - What obstacle did Andrew address?
   - What obstacle did Philip address?
   - What obstacles are you facing in your overwhelming situation?
   - What needs to be moved out of the way in order for you to overcome these obstacles?
   - Do you believe you have any power over these obstacles? Why or why not?

5. Regarding the doubting disciples, Max says, "They counted the hungry people, the money in their bag, and the amount of bread and fish. They did not, however, count on _____" (p. 53). Fill in the blank.
   • Even though the disciples knew Jesus, believed in him, and had seen him perform miracles, why do you think they didn't turn to Christ for the solution in this situation?
   • Think of a time you turned to Christ for a solution to your overwhelming problem. Explain the problem and solution.

6. Read John 6:11–13.
   • How did Jesus meet the needs of the crowd?
   • How much was everyone able to eat?
   • What does the fact that there were leftovers tell you about Jesus and this miracle?

7. Max says this miracle proves that "what we cannot do, Christ does! The problems we face are opportunities for Christ to prove this point" (p. 54).
   • What do you think about this statement?
   • In the past has Christ solved a problem for you in a way you couldn't have done yourself? If so, how did Christ do this?
   • Do you believe he can solve your problem today? Why or why not?

8. Believing that Christ will solve your problem requires creativity, as all problem-solving does. It requires that you see

things not simply as they are but as they could be. Do an exercise in creativity with whatever overwhelming situation or problem you are facing today. List below the possible outcomes that feel impossible today. List good, profitable, positive things that could happen as a result of your problem. It doesn't matter how crazy it is—a healed body, a reconciled relationship, a new job you love. Just write it down, and open your heart and mind to what is possible through Jesus.

CHAPTER 6

I AM in the Storm with You

1. Max opens this chapter with a heartbreaking story of abuse from his childhood. When he took Communion in his kitchen that night, what gave him a sense of peace?
   • Have you felt the presence of God during a dark moment?
   • If so, how did you know it was the presence of God, and how did his presence make you feel?
   • If you haven't sought God's presence during a dark moment, where did you turn for help? What kept you from seeking God's help?

2. Fill in the blank: "Jesus comes in the _____ of the torrent" (p. 60). The miracle you read about in this chapter proves this, literally. Read John 6:14–17.
   • What were the disciples doing in these verses?
   • Where was Jesus?

3. Now read John 6:18–19. How far had the disciples rowed when they saw Jesus approaching?

According to Matthew 14:24 (NKJV) the disciples had rowed to the middle of the Sea of Galilee. There was no turning back to get safely to shore. They had to stay in the storm or hope they made it to the other side.

• What storms have you endured?

• How did you feel in the midst of them?

• How were these storms eventually calmed?

• Perhaps you are in a storm right now. What is the source of your storm? Like the disciples, are you in the middle of a lake, helpless as the seas rage around you? Or has this storm just started? Or are the waters beginning to calm?

4. Max points out three different struggles we encounter in a storm: too far from shore (the solution), too long in the struggle, and too small against the waves (the problem). Which one of these have you struggled with before or are struggling with today in your storm?

5. John 6:19 says, "They saw Jesus approaching the boat, walking on the water; and they were frightened" (NIV). Put yourself in this scene. Imagine you are a disciple trying to row the boat to safety. How would you feel on a small boat, in the middle of a big lake, in the middle of a storm?

Now imagine you see your beloved rabbi. But he is not in the boat or on the shore. He is on the water. Walking.

• What mix of emotions would you feel at the sight of Christ in this moment?

• What kind of thoughts would be going through your head, and why?

6. Jesus, anticipating the disciples' confusion, announced himself by saying, "It is I; don't be afraid" (John 6:20 NIV).
   - What does Max say is the literal translation of "It is I"? (See p. 63.)
   - Why is this significant?
   - Right after Jesus told the disciples who he is, what did he tell them?
   - How do you think the disciples felt when Jesus told them not to be afraid?

7. What does Max say is our greatest need during a storm? (See p. 63.) Do you agree with this? Why or why not?

8. Read John 6:21. What happened when the disciples let Jesus onto their boat?

9. Max suggests an interesting scenario on page 64. Imagine welcoming Jesus into a turbulent period of your life. What would Jesus notice? What do you think he might say or do?
   - In the past have you asked Jesus to join you in your storm?
   - If so, how did the presence of Jesus alter your chaos, despair, or pain?
   - Have you hesitated to invite Jesus into your difficult moments and seasons?
   - What would you need to believe about Jesus, his character, or his power in order to welcome him into your storm?

10. Max tells the story of Katherine Wolf, a former model who suffered a massive stroke that left her severely debilitated. Although she still struggles with her health, she has encountered God in her storm, and her heart and mind are stronger than ever. If the circumstances of your storm stayed the same but you welcomed Christ in the midst of them, would anything change for you? If so, what?

11. Read Isaiah 43:1–3, 5 again on page 63. Which of the promises made in this scripture do you need most today, and why?

CHAPTER 7

He Gives Sight to the Blind

1. Compared to the other miracles recorded by John that you've read so far, what is different about the way John wrote the miracle story discussed in this chapter? Why would John have done this?

2. Fill in the blanks: "What Jesus did physically for the blind beggar, he desires to do _____ for all people: restore our _____" (p. 70).
   - Have you experienced this type of spiritual sight? Perhaps when you were converted or understood a deeper truth about Jesus? If so, describe what that moment was like.
   - What had you been blind to until that point?
   - What was it like to see in a new way?
   - Maybe you haven't experienced this in your faith but elsewhere in your life. Have you ever come to a deeper understanding about something or someone that opened your eyes? If so, explain what that experience was like.

- What did it take for you to see clearly?
- How can that experience guide you to a deeper faith?

3. Read John 9:1–2. What is the difference between how the disciples viewed the blind man and how Jesus viewed him? Max says this difference presents the first lesson we can learn from this miracle. What is that lesson?

4. Read John 9:3–7. How did Jesus heal the blind man?
   - Why do you think he chose to heal him in this way?
   - What "mud moments"—difficult lessons that led to better understanding—have you experienced in your life?
   - How did you feel while the metaphorical mud was on your eyes?
   - How did you feel when it was removed?
   - Why do you think God teaches us in this way?
   - Perhaps you are in a "mud moment" right now. What do you think Jesus could be planning to reveal to you?

5. Jesus continued this healing miracle by asking the blind man to wash his face in the pool of Siloam (John 9:7). Max points out that the walk to the pool for a blind man would have been difficult (p. 74). Why do you think the blind man went anyway?
   - Has God ever asked you to do something difficult and you didn't know why?
   - If so, did you obey or resist? What happened as a result?
   - What does this part of the story tell you about the character of the blind man?

6. Read John 9:13–20. How did the Pharisees respond to the blind man's healing?
   - How did the blind man respond to the Pharisees?
   - When you've had your eyes opened spiritually, have people in your life been skeptical of your new worldview or understanding?
   - If so, why do you think they were skeptical?
   - How did their doubts make you feel? What did you say, if anything, to defend yourself and your experience?

7. The Pharisees eventually threw the blind man out of the synagogue. This was significant and would have affected the blind man's ability to worship in his community. Why do you think the Pharisees took it this far?
   - Can you think of any examples of church leaders shunning someone for telling a truth that was uncomfortable or threatening to them?
   - Why does the truth sometimes feel offensive?

8. Read John 9:35–41. Ultimately how did this miracle affect the blind man beyond giving him physical sight?
   - Even though he had been cast out of his religious community for talking about Jesus' power, the blind man still talked to Jesus when Jesus found him, and the blind man believed in Jesus as the Son of God. Why do you think he believed in Jesus?
   - According to Jesus in verse 41, what made the Pharisees guilty?
   - Have you been guilty of claiming you understood

something only to realize later that you didn't understand? If so, what did you misunderstand? What or who opened your eyes?

• Is God challenging you on something in your life today? Perhaps you think you understand something or someone but God is pushing you to a deeper or different understanding. Explain. Could you ask God to help you understand this through the perspective of Christ?

9. Of the lessons you learned from this miracle, which one was most helpful to you today, and why?

CHAPTER 8

The Voice That Empties Graves

1. Death is a reality that affects everyone. When you think about death, what is your perspective? Are you afraid of it? In denial of it? At peace with it? Curious about it? Trying to beat it? Why?

2. Has someone close to you passed away? If so, how did this affect your attitude and thoughts about death? Did it cause you to consider your own eventual passing?

3. Read John 11:1–6.
   • How did Mary and Martha refer to Lazarus in their message to Jesus?
   • What do you think they were hoping Jesus would do in response to their message?
   • What did Jesus do instead?
   • What was Jesus' reason for his action?

4. Have you ever asked God to do something—heal someone,

change your circumstances, or something else—and he didn't do it?

- How did that make you feel about the circumstances?
- How did that make you feel about God?

5. Read John 11:11–15. Jesus knew what was happening with Lazarus. It wasn't ignorance that kept Jesus from visiting sooner. He was not surprised by Lazarus's death. What do you think it was like for Jesus to allow his dear friend to die when he could have stopped it?

- What does this tell you about the purpose and importance of this miracle?
- What does this tell you about the circumstances you are praying for but haven't received an answer for yet?

6. John 11:20 says, "When Martha got word that Jesus was coming, she went to meet him. But Mary stayed in the house" (NLT). Why would Mary have stayed in the house instead of going to greet Jesus?

- What would you have done if you were Mary or Martha?
- Has Jesus responded to one of your prayers with an answer you considered too little and too late? What had you been praying for, and how did you hope Jesus would answer it?
- Did Jesus' response affect your faith? If so, in what ways?

7. Read John 11:28–33. What did Mary say to Jesus when she finally went to him (v. 32)?

- What do you think of Mary's words to Jesus?
- How did Jesus respond to Mary?
- Why do you think Jesus was angry?
- When you read of Jesus' weeping, what does that reveal about his depth of compassion for you?
- What do Jesus' emotions in these verses tell you about who he was and is?

8. Max describes the moment Jesus told Lazarus to come out of the grave as a command, not an invitation (p. 87). In what ways did this moment display Jesus' power?

9. Max points out that besides Jesus' power to raise the dead to life, this miracle makes us another promise. What is it? (See p. 89.)

10. Lazarus is described as Jesus' "dear friend." You may not think Jesus considers you to be his dear friend too, but read the following verses that describe our relationship to God through Christ:

> 1 Peter 2:9: "But you are a chosen generation, a royal priesthood, a holy nation, His own special people, that you may proclaim the praises of Him who called you out of darkness into His marvelous light."

> Ephesians 2:10: "For we are His workmanship, created in Christ Jesus for good works, which God prepared beforehand that we should walk in them."

Romans 8:15–17: "So you have not received a spirit that makes you fearful slaves. Instead, you received God's Spirit when he adopted you as his own children. Now we call him, 'Abba, Father.' For his Spirit joins with our spirit to affirm that we are God's children. And since we are his children, we are his heirs. In fact, together with Christ we are heirs of God's glory" (NLT).

- Underline each word that describes how God sees us.
- Which of these descriptions resonates with you the most? Why?
- Which of these descriptions are hard for you to believe about yourself? Why?
- Since Jesus raised his dear friend Lazarus from the dead, how eager do you think he is to include us—God's workmanship, children, and heirs—in the resurrection one day?

11. Jesus made a bold proclamation and asked a pointed question in John 11:25–26: "I am the resurrection and the life. Anyone who believes in me will live, even after dying. Everyone who lives in me and believes in me will never ever die. Do you believe this, Martha?" (NLT). Replace Martha's name with your own. Do you believe this? Why or why not?

CHAPTER 9

Paid in Full

1. Before reading this chapter, what did you know about the crucifixion of Christ? What did you believe was the purpose of Jesus' dying on the cross?

2. Why does Max say the crucifixion can be considered a miracle?

3. Jesus' final words from the cross were "It is finished!" (John 19:30). The Greek word translated as "it is finished" is *tetelestai*. What is significant about Jesus' using this particular word in this context?

4. Max poses the question, "Exactly what was finished?" (p. 99). How would you answer this?

5. What sin or circumstance from your past still makes you feel guilt or shame? Why is this guilt or shame so strong?

6. Citing Hebrews 10:14 ("For by one offering He [Christ] has

perfected forever those who are being sanctified"), Max says, "No further offering is needed. Heaven awaits no additional sacrifice" (p. 99).

- What thoughts arise when you read those words?
- Do you fully believe in the power of Jesus' final offering?
- Does the way you feel about your own sin reflect this belief? Why or why not?

7. It is easy to forget the promise "It is finished." We often try to earn our forgiveness by making our own offerings. Have you ever done this? If so, how have you tried to make your own offerings for your sin and mistakes?

8. Some people find it difficult to accept Christ's atoning sacrifice. Guilt hinders a ready acceptance. Have you readily received this gift, or is guilt holding you back from accepting "the great miracle of mercy"?

9. Read the following verses:

    1 Corinthians 6:18: "Flee sexual immorality. Every sin that a man does is outside the body, but he who commits sexual immorality sins against his own body."

    Galatians 5:19–21: "Now the works of the flesh are evident, which are: adultery, fornication, uncleanness, lewdness, idolatry, sorcery, hatred, contentions, jealousies, outbursts of wrath, selfish ambitions, dissensions, heresies, envy, murders, drunkenness, revelries, and the like; of which I tell you beforehand, just as I also told you in time past, that those who practice such things will not inherit the kingdom of God."

Colossians 3:5–7: "Therefore put to death your members which are on the earth: fornication, uncleanness, passion, evil desire, and covetousness, which is idolatry. Because of these things the wrath of God is coming upon the sons of disobedience, in which you yourselves once walked when you lived in them."

• What is the common warning in these verses?
• Do you feel tension or confusion with any of these verses? If so, which ones, and why?

Now read the following verses:

Psalm 103:10–13: "He doesn't treat us as our sins deserve, nor pay us back in full for our wrongs. As high as heaven is over the earth, so strong is his love to those who fear him. And as far as sunrise is from sunset, he has separated us from our sins. As parents feel for their children, GOD feels for those who fear him" (THE MESSAGE).

Romans 8:38–39: "For I am persuaded that neither death nor life, nor angels nor principalities nor powers, nor things present nor things to come, nor height nor depth, nor any other created thing, shall be able to separate us from the love of God which is in Christ Jesus our Lord."

Romans 6:6–7: "For we know that our old self was crucified with him so that the body ruled by sin might be done away with, that we should no longer be slaves to sin—because anyone who has died has been set free from sin" (NIV).

- What is the common theme in these passages?
- How do we balance accepting the full forgiveness of our sins while still, as Scripture encourages us to do, striving not to sin?

10. Return to your answer to question 5. Do you feel any different about this sin, mistake, or circumstance in light of understanding more about the crucifixion? If so, how? If not, why not?

11. Max tells the story of his granddaughter Rosie seeing the ocean for the first time. She asked when the ocean would turn off. Max said, "It doesn't, sweetie." If you truly believed that God's grace was never-ending like the oceans' tides, how would it affect your life?
- How would it change the way you interact with others?
- How might it alter the way you view yourself?

CHAPTER 10

He Saw and Believed

1. Which of the following best describes you and your faith today, and why? (FYI: There is no wrong answer.)

   Fervent believer: You are a firm believer in Jesus as God's Son, who was crucified, buried, and rose again to new life.

   Hopeful skeptic: You're not entirely sure about Jesus and the resurrection, but you are seeking and hopeful about faith and spirituality.

   Nonbeliever: Jesus is a respected historical figure, but he was not raised from the dead.

2. At the beginning of this chapter, Max confesses a time when he doubted the resurrection of Christ. If you consider yourself a "fervent believer," have you ever doubted this or something else about the Christian faith? If so, what have you doubted, and why?

   If you identify as a hopeful skeptic or nonbeliever, what do you doubt about the story of Jesus, and why?

3. In your faith or church background, was it permissible to have doubts?
   - How did these feelings and doubts affect your faith journey?
   - Do you think it's okay to doubt your faith or for others to doubt? Why or why not?

4. Read John 19:38–41. How was Jesus' body prepared? Where was his body placed?

5. Now read John 20:1–8. What did John and Peter find in the tomb? Why is this significant?

6. When was the moment John first believed that Jesus had been raised from the dead? (See John 20:8.)
   - Why did John believe Jesus had been raised from the dead even though he hadn't yet seen Jesus alive?
   - What evidence did John have that Jesus was alive?

7. When was the moment you first believed in Jesus' resurrection?
   - What caused you to believe? Evidence? Faith? Both?
   - What did this belief mean for you?
   - How did this belief change you?
   - What did it feel like to believe?

8. How many times did John use the word *believe* in his gospel?
   - Why do you think he used it so often?
   - Max says, "*Believe* means more than mere credence. It signifies _____ ____ and _____ __" (p. 109). Fill in the blanks.

- Would you say you have this type of belief in the resurrection? Why or why not?

9. Why is belief in the resurrection of Christ so important to the Christian faith?
   - Do you consider the resurrection central to your belief? Why or why not?
   - Do you think it's possible to be a Christian but not believe in the resurrection? Why or why not?
   - First Corinthians 15:17 says, "If Christ has not been raised, your faith is worthless and powerless" (AMP). Why is that? Do you feel any points of tension with this passage?

10. What further evidence for the truth of the resurrection does Max suggest? (See p. 111.)
    - Why is the number of witnesses to Christ's death and resurrection so significant?
    - Think about how history has been recorded over the years through eyewitness accounts and documentation. We believe what we read in history books. What keeps us, or others, from believing what the Bible says about the resurrection?
    - Is there any difference between believing in the history you were taught in school and believing in Christ's resurrection? If so, what is that difference?

11. John first saw the risen Christ on the evening he was resurrected. Read John 20:19–22.

- What were Jesus' first words to the disciples?
- What did he show them?
- How did this make the disciples feel?
- Having seen the empty tomb and burial linens, what was John probably thinking and feeling in this moment?

12. Max writes, "Faith is not the absence of doubt. Faith is simply a willingness to keep asking the hard questions" (p. 113). What hard questions do you need to ask God today? Maybe you have some questions about the resurrection or perhaps about something happening in your life. Or maybe you have some doubts about other areas of your faith. Whatever it is, bring your questions and doubts to the Father. Bring them without shame or fear, because he understands and wants to listen.

CHAPTER 11

Breakfast with Jesus

1. Have you broken a promise to a loved one?
   - What promise did you break?
   - How did your loved one respond to the broken promise?
   - If he or she forgave you, how did that change your relationship?
   - If he or she held it against you, what actions or changes resulted?

2. We've all hurt the people in our lives. And we've all hurt God. As Max writes, "We, too, have fallen flat, fallen hard, and fallen enough to leave us wondering how in God's name God names us as his own. I'm not talking about minor slip-ups. . . . I'm calling to the surface the Jonah moments in which we turned from God, Elijah moments in which we ran from God, Jacob moments in which we dared to make a demand of God" (p. 119).
   - When you read this, what comes to mind about a time you fell and fell hard?

- How do you think God feels about this event or time in your life?

3. Max describes Peter's relationship with Jesus as a Rocky Mountain friendship. Read Luke 5:1–11.
   - How did the relationship between Peter and Jesus begin?
   - How did Peter react to Jesus in verse 8?
   - What did Peter and the other disciples do in verse 11?
   - How would you describe Peter's relationship with Jesus, based on this passage?
   - Describe a time, if any, that your relationship with Jesus was like this—new, exciting, and real, so real that you were willing to do anything for him.

4. Read Mark 14:27–31.
   - What did Peter vow to Jesus in this passage?
   - Do you think Peter meant what he said? Why or why not?
   - How would you describe Peter's relationship with Jesus, based on this passage?
   - Have you ever made a similar promise to Jesus? If so, what was the promise, and why did you make it?

5. Read Mark 14:66–72.
   - Why do you think Peter denied his relationship with Jesus?
   - What did Peter do after the cock crowed and Peter recalled Jesus' words?

- Have you ever broken a promise you made to Jesus? Perhaps the same promise you listed in question 4?
- How did you feel when you realized you had broken your promise?

6. In Mark 16:7 the angel of the Lord mentioned Peter, and only Peter, by name among the disciples. Max says, "It's as if all of heaven had watched Peter fall. Now all of heaven wanted to help him back on his feet."
   - What does this tell you about Jesus and how he felt about Peter?
   - What does this tell you about how Jesus feels about you?

7. Read John 21:1–9.
   - What similarities are there between the story of this miracle and the story in Luke 5:1–11?
   - Now read John 21:15–17. How does this conversation parallel Peter's denial of Christ in Mark 14:66–72?
   - What do you think is the significance of these similarities in Scripture?
   - What do they say about Peter's relationship with Jesus?

8. Of all the scenarios of Peter you just read, which one most resonates with you today?
   - Are you a new believer, willing to give up everything for Jesus?
   - Have you made a promise to Jesus?
   - Have you broken that promise and now are dealing with the shame?

- Or have you recently experienced the deep forgiveness of Christ and a restored relationship with him?
- Regardless of where you stand today, what would you like your relationship with Jesus to look like?

9. Max tells the story of his wife forgiving him. What message of forgiveness do you need Jesus to write on your mirror?

10. Peter's duties were not done. Jesus told him, "Feed My lambs. . . . Tend My sheep. . . . Feed My sheep" (John 21:15–17).
   - What work did Peter go on to do for Christ? (See p. 127.)
   - Have you let your failure keep you from believing you can continue working for Christ?
   - If so, what do you believe you aren't equipped to do anymore?
   - If you felt fully forgiven by Jesus, what work would you want to do in his name?

11. Max points out that Jesus offered Peter forgiveness, but Peter had to take a step toward it. Peter went to Galilee, he jumped into the water and swam to shore, and he talked to Jesus. Do you need to take a step toward Jesus today? If so, what would that look like for you?

CHAPTER 12

Believe, Just Believe

1. John recorded the reason for his gospel and for telling about the signs and wonders of Christ: "But these are written that you may believe that Jesus is the Messiah, the Son of God, and that by believing you may have life in his name" (John 20:31 NIV). How has studying the miracles of Jesus affected your belief in him as the resurrected Son of God?

2. What truth or promise did you take away from each miracle listed below? Which one seemed most in tune with your life today?

   When Jesus turned the water into wine:

   When he healed the nobleman's son:

   When he healed the lame man:

   When he healed the blind man:

   When he walked on water:

   When he fed the five thousand:

   When he raised Lazarus from the dead:

   When he completed the work of redemption on the cross:

   When his body was resurrected:

When he multiplied the fish in the disciples' net and gave Peter a second chance:

3. Max writes, "The message of the miracles is the Miracle Worker himself. He wants you to know you are never alone. You are never without help, hope, or strength. You are stronger than you think because God is nearer than you might imagine" (p. 138). Of the miracles listed above, which one most assures you of this promise, and why?

4. Max tells the touching story of Luke making a shot in a basketball game after his teammates and even the opposing team threw the ball to him again and again.
   - How are we like Luke in this scenario?
   - Think about the past week. Did you experience any miracles that you overlooked in the moment? If so, what were they?
   - What miracles have others around you experienced that you have failed to see as a miracle?
   - Why is it difficult for us to notice the miracles happening around us each day?
   - Do you typically call such events miracles or something else, like a coincidence or stroke of fate? Why?
   - What do these miracles in your life—big or small—tell you about God and his presence?

5. Max lists several passages of Scripture that assure us of the nearness of God (p. 138). Which of these passages do you most need to believe today, and why?

6. The first question in the first chapter of these reflection questions was "What do you think about miracles?" Has your answer to this changed in any way, or has it stayed the same? Explain why.

7. What doubts do you still have about miracles, either in your own life or the miracles recorded in the gospel of John?
   • Why do you have these specific doubts?
   • What would you need to see or experience to overcome these doubts?

8. The ultimate promise of this book is the title: *You Are Never Alone.* How can this promise change you, your life, your faith, and your relationships?

9. Take any final thoughts, questions, prayers, or concerns to the Father. If you need a miracle in your life, ask for it. If you need more faith, ask for it. If you need forgiveness, ask for it. If you need to know you are never alone, ask God for a strong, peaceful sense of his never-ending presence.

Notes

Chapter 1

1. "The 'Loneliness Epidemic," https://www.hrsa.gov/enews/past
   -issues/2019/january-17/loneliness-epidemic; Julianne Holt-Lunstad,
   PhD, "The Potential Public Health Relevance of Social Isolation
   and Loneliness: Prevalence, Epidemiology, and Risk Factors,"
   Public Policy & Aging Report, volume 27, issue 4, 2017, pages
   127–130, https://doi.org/10.1093/ppar/prx030, published January
   2, 2018; "Friends are Healthy—Impact of Loneliness on Health &
   Cognition," https://www.themaples-towson.com/news/friends-are
   -healthy-impact-of-lonliness-on-health-cognition.
2. Teresa Woodard, "80 People Went to Dallas Emergency Rooms
   5,139 Times in a Year—Usually Because They Were Lonely,"
   WFAA, May 28, 2019, https://www.wfaa.com/article/features
   /originals/80-people-went-to-dallas-emergency-rooms-5139-times
   -in-a-year-usually-because-they-were-lonely/287-f5351d53–6e60–
   4d64–8d17–6ebba48a01e4.

Chapter 2

1. "This is where faith stands in the heat of battle. . . . [Mary] does not in her heart interpret this as anger, or as the opposite of kindness, but adheres firmly to the conviction that he [Jesus] is kind . . . unwilling to dishonor him in her heart by thinking him to be otherwise than kind and gracious. . . . Hence the highest thought in this Gospel lesson, and it must ever be kept in mind, is, that we honor God as being good and gracious, even if he acts and speaks otherwise. . . . She is certain that he will be gracious, although she does not feel it." Martin Luther as quoted in Frederick Dale Bruner, *The Gospel of John: A Commentary* (Grand Rapids, MI: Eerdmans, 2012), 138–39.

2. Six water jars of 25 gallons each equals 150 gallons. There are 128 ounces in a gallon, so 150 gallons would equal 19,200 ounces. A wine bottle typically holds 25.4 ounces, so 19,200 ounces would fill 756 bottles.

Chapter 3

1. Bill Bryson, *A Walk in the Woods: Rediscovering America on the Appalachian Trail* (New York: Random House, 1998), 161.

2. Zach C. Cohen, "Bill Irwin Dies at 73; First Blind Hiker of Appalachian Trail," *Washington Post*, March 15, 2014, https://www.washingtonpost.com/national/bill-irwin-dies-at-73-first -blind-hiker-of-appalachian-trail/2014/03/15/a12cfa1a-ab9b-11e3 -af5f-4c56b834c4bf_story.html.

3. R. Kent Hughes, *John: That You May Believe* (Wheaton, IL: Crossway, 1999), 138.

Chapter 4

1. Grace Murano, "10 Bizarre Stories of People Getting Stuck," Oddee, April 4, 2011, https:// www.oddee.com/item_97665.aspx.

2. More recent translations of this passage have chosen to remove a curious reference to an angel who would, on occasion, stir the surface. The first person to touch the water after the bubbles appeared would be healed. Almost all evangelical scholars agree that these words were added by a redactor or editor who wanted to explain why people came to the pool. Whether the phrase was a

part of John's original text or not, the fact remains that the pool of Bethesda was encircled by crowds of sick people—"Blind, lame, or paralyzed [that] lay on the porches" (John 5:3).

3. "Bethesda," BibleWalks.com, https://biblewalks.com/Sites/Bethesda.html.
4. Lee Strobel, *The Case for Miracles: A Journalist Investigates Evidence for the Supernatural* (Grand Rapids, MI: Zondervan, 2018), 101–4. Billy Hallowell, "The Real-Life Miracle That Absolutely Shocked Lee Strobel," Pure Flix.com, April 24, 2018, https://insider.pureflix.com/movies/the-real-life-miracle-that-absolutely-shocked-lee-strobel.
5. Used by permission.

Chapter 5

1. Translation by Frederick Dale Bruner, *The Gospel of John: A Commentary* (Grand Rapids, MI: Eerdmans, 2012), 359.
2. Bruner, *Gospel of John*, 359.
3. Bruner, 359.
4. Gen. 41:9–14; Ex. 2:6; 1 Sam. 17:48–49; Matt. 27:32–54.
5. "Chambers, Gertrude (Biddy) (1884–1966); Archival Collections at Wheaton College," Wheaton College, https://archon.wheaton.edu/index.php?p=creators/creator&id=198.
6. Macy Halford, "Why We're Still Reading 'My Utmost for His Highest' 80 Years Later," *Christianity Today,* March 9, 2017, https://www.christianitytoday.com/ct/2017/march-web-only/utmost-for-his-highest-popular-devotional-reading-chambers.html.

Chapter 6

1. In case you're curious, the perpetrator's secret caught up with him, and he was punished for his actions.
2. Katherine and Jay Wolf, *Hope Heals: A True Story of Overwhelming Loss and an Overcoming Love* (Grand Rapids, MI: Zondervan, 2016), 163–65.

Chapter 7

1. John Newton, "Amazing Grace," Timeless Truths, https://library.timelesstruths.org/music/Amazing_Grace/.

2. Lea Winerman, "By the Numbers: An Alarming Rise in Suicide," *American Psychological Association* 50, no. 1 (January 2019), https://www.apa.org/monitor/2019/01/numbers.

3. "Opioid Overdose Crisis," National Institute on Drug Abuse, NIH, revised February 2020, https://www.drugabuse.gov/drugs-abuse /opioids/opioid-overdose-crisis.

4. John 3:17; 4:34; 5:24, 30, 36; 6:29, 38, 44, 57; 7:16, 18, 28, 29, 33; 8:16, 18, 26, 29, 42; 9:4.

5. Hershel Shanks, "The Siloam Pool: Where Jesus Cured the Blind Man," *Biblical Archaeology Review* 31:5 (Sept/Oct 2005), baslibrary.org/biblical-archaeology-review/31/5/2.

6. Lee Strobel, *The Case for Miracles: A Journalist Investigates Evidence for the Supernatural* (Grand Rapids, MI: Zondervan, 2018), 141.

7. Tom Doyle, *Dreams and Visions: Is Jesus Awakening the Muslim World?* (Nashville: Thomas Nelson, 2012), 127.

8. Strobel, *Case for Miracles,* 146.

9. Strobel, 152.

10. The exception is the healing of Saul by Ananias (Acts 9:8–18).

11. C. H. Spurgeon, *The Metropolitan Tabernacle Pulpit: Sermons Preached and Revised in 1884* (London: Banner of Truth Trust, 1971), 30:489.

Chapter 8

1. Frederick Dale Bruner, *The Gospel of John: A Commentary* (Grand Rapids, MI: Eerdmans, 2012), 664.

2. Bruner, *Gospel of John,* 681.

3. Used with permission of Russ Levenson.

Chapter 9

1. Used with permission of Kayla Montgomery.

Chapter 10

1. Some Bible versions say about one hundred pounds. Other versions say about seventy or seventy-five pounds.

2. William Barclay, *The Gospel of John,* rev. ed. (Philadelphia: Westminster Press, 1975), 2:263.

3. Gary M. Burge, *John*, The NIV Application Commentary (Grand Rapids, MI: Zondervan, 2000), 554.
4. Edward W. Goodrick and John R. Kohlenberger III, *The NIV Exhaustive Concordance* (Grand Rapids, MI: Zondervan, 1990), 127–28.
5. "The grave-clothes were not dishevelled and disarranged. They were lying there *still in their folds*." Barclay, *Gospel of John*, 2:267.
6. Arthur W. Pink, *Exposition of the Gospel of John* (Grand Rapids, MI: Zondervan, 1945), 1:1077.
7. Burge, *John*, 554.
8. John Stott says the body of Christ "vaporized, being transmuted into something new and different and wonderful." John Stott, *Basic Christianity* (Downers Grove, IL: InterVarsity, 1959), 53.

Chapter 11
1. Ross King, *Leonardo and the Last Supper* (New York: Bloomsbury, 2012), 271–73.

Chapter 12
1. Used by permission.
2. Used by permission.
3. Mark Bouman, *The Tank Man's Son: A Memoir* (Carol Stream, IL: Tyndale, 2015), 316–18, 333–34.

The Lucado Reader's Guide

Discover . . . Inside every book by Max Lucado, you'll find words of encouragement and inspiration that will draw you into a deeper experience with Jesus and treasures for your walk with God. What will you discover?

3:16: The Numbers of Hope
... the 26 words that can change your life.
core scripture: John 3:16

And the Angels Were Silent
... what Jesus Christ's final days can teach you about what matters most.
core scripture: Matthew 20–27

Anxious for Nothing
... be anxious for nothing.
core scripture: Philippians 4:4–8

The Applause of Heaven
... the secret to a truly satisfying life.
core scripture: The Beatitudes, Matthew 5:1–10

Before Amen
... the power of a simple prayer.
core scripture: Psalm 145:19

Come Thirsty
... how to rehydrate your heart and sink into the wellspring of God's love.
core scripture: John 7:37–38

Cure for the Common Life
... the unique things God designed you to do with your life.
core scripture: 1 Corinthians 12:7

Facing Your Giants
... when God is for you, no challenge is too great.
core scripture: 1 and 2 Samuel

Fearless
... how faith is the antidote to the fear in your life.
core scripture: John 14:1, 3

A Gentle Thunder
... the God who will do whatever it takes to lead his children back to him.
core scripture: Psalm 81:7

Glory Days
... how you fight from victory, not for it.
core scripture: Joshua 21:43–45

God Came Near
... a love so great that it left heaven to become part of your world.
core scripture: John 1:14

Grace
... the incredible gift that saves and sustains you.
core scripture: Hebrews 12:15

The Great House of God
... a blueprint for peace, joy, and love found in the Lord's Prayer.
core scripture: The Lord's Prayer, Matthew 6:9–13

He Chose the Nails
... a love so deep that it chose death on a cross—just to win your heart.
core scripture: 1 Peter 1:18–20

He Still Moves Stones
... the God who still does the impossible—in your life.
core scripture: Matthew 12:20

In the Eye of the Storm
... peace in the storms of your life.
core scripture: John 6

In the Grip of Grace
... the greatest gift of all—the grace of God.
core scripture: Romans

It's Not About Me
... why focusing on God will make sense of your life.
core scripture: 2 Corinthians 3:18

Just Like Jesus
... a life free from guilt, fear, and anxiety.
core scripture: Ephesians 4:23–24

A Love Worth Giving
... how living loved frees you to love others.
core scripture: 1 Corinthians 13

Next Door Savior
... a God who walked life's hardest trials—and still walks with you through yours.
core scripture: Matthew 16:13–16

No Wonder They Call Him the Savior
... hope in the unlikeliest place—upon the cross.
core scripture: Romans 5:15

Outlive Your Life
... that a great God created you to do great things.
core scripture: Acts 1

Six Hours One Friday
... forgiveness and healing in the middle of loss and failure.
core scripture: John 19–20

Traveling Light
... the power to release the burdens you were never meant to carry.
core scripture: Psalm 23

Unshakable Hope
... God has given us his very great and precious promises.
core scripture: 2 Peter 1:4

When God Whispers Your Name
... the path to hope in knowing that God knows you, never forgets you, and cares about the details of your life.
core scripture: John 10:3

You'll Get Through This
... hope in the midst of your hard times and a God who uses the mess of life for good.
core scripture: Genesis 50:20

Recommended reading if you're struggling with . . .

FEAR AND WORRY

Anxious for Nothing
Before Amen
Come Thirsty
Fearless
For the Tough Times
Next Door Savior
Traveling Light

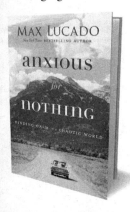

DISCOURAGEMENT

He Still Moves Stones
Next Door Savior

GRIEF/DEATH OF A LOVED ONE

Next Door Savior
Traveling Light
When Christ Comes
When God Whispers Your Name
You'll Get Through This

GUILT

In the Grip of Grace
Just Like Jesus

LONELINESS

God Came Near

SIN

Before Amen
Facing Your Giants
He Chose the Nails
Six Hours One Friday

WEARINESS

Before Amen
When God Whispers Your Name
You'll Get Through This

Recommended reading if you want to know more about . . .

THE CROSS

And the Angels Were Silent
He Chose the Nails
No Wonder They Call Him the Savior
Six Hours One Friday

GRACE

Before Amen
Grace
He Chose the Nails
In the Grip of Grace

HEAVEN

The Applause of Heaven
When Christ Comes

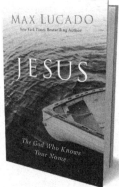

SHARING THE GOSPEL

God Came Near
Grace
No Wonder They Call Him the Savior

Recommended reading if you're looking for more . . .

COMFORT

For the Tough Times
He Chose the Nails
Next Door Savior
Traveling Light
You'll Get Through This

COMPASSION

Outlive Your Life

COURAGE

Facing Your Giants
Fearless

HOPE

3:16: The Numbers of Hope
Before Amen
Facing Your Giants
A Gentle Thunder
God Came Near
Grace
Unshakable Hope

JOY

The Applause of Heaven
Cure for the Common Life
When God Whispers Your Name

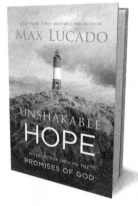

LOVE

Come Thirsty
A Love Worth Giving
No Wonder They Call Him the Savior

PEACE

And the Angels Were Silent
Anxious for Nothing
Before Amen
The Great House of God
In the Eye of the Storm
Traveling Light
You'll Get Through This

SATISFACTION

And the Angels Were Silent
Come Thirsty
Cure for the Common Life
Great Day Every Day

TRUST

A Gentle Thunder
It's Not About Me
Next Door Savior

Max Lucado books make great gifts!
If you're coming up to a special occasion, consider one of these.

FOR ADULTS:

Anxious for Nothing
For the Tough Times
Grace for the Moment
Live Loved
The Lucado Life Lessons Study Bible
Mocha with Max
DaySpring Daybrighteners® and cards

FOR TEENS/GRADUATES:

Let the Journey Begin
You Can Be Everything God Wants You to Be
You Were Made to Make a Difference

FOR KIDS:

I'm Not a Scaredy Cat
Just in Case You Ever Wonder
The Oak Inside the Acorn
You Are Special

FOR PASTORS AND TEACHERS:

God Thinks You're Wonderful
You Changed My Life

AT CHRISTMAS:

Because of Bethlehem
The Crippled Lamb
The Christmas Candle
God Came Near

NEW VIDEO STUDY FOR YOUR CHURCH OR SMALL GROUP

If you've enjoyed this book, now you can go deeper with the companion video Bible study!

In this six-session study, Max Lucado helps you apply the principles in *You Are Never Alone* to your life. The study guide includes video notes, group discussion questions, and personal study and reflection materials for in-between sessions.

Study Guide
9780310115557

DVD with Free Streaming
9780310115571

Available now at your favorite bookstore,
or streaming video on StudyGateway.com.

THOMAS NELSON
Since 1798

Inspired by what you just read?
Connect with Max.

Listen to Max's teaching ministry, UpWords, on the radio and online. Visit www.MaxLucado.com to get FREE resources for spiritual growth and encouragement, including:

- Archives of *UpWords*, Max's daily radio program, and a list of radio stations where it airs
- Devotionals and e-mails from Max
- First look at book excerpts
- Downloads of audio, video, and printed material
- Mobile content

You will also find an online store and special offers.

www.MaxLucado.com

1-800-822-9673

UpWords Ministries
P.O. Box 692170
San Antonio, TX 78269-2170

Join the Max Lucado community:
Facebook.com/MaxLucado
Instagram.com/MaxLucado
Twitter.com/MaxLucado